A Guide to
Crawford Notch

A locomotive, passing over Willey Brook Bridge, works its way south through Crawford Notch a century ago.

A Guide to Crawford Notch

MIKE DICKERMAN

with John Dickerman & Steven D. Smith

Bondcliff Books
Littleton, N.H.

A Guide to Crawford Notch

Published by Bondcliff Books,

Littleton, NH

Library of Congress Catalog Card Number 97-71040

ISBN 0-9657475-0-6

Text and cover design by Tim Leavitt
Printed in the United States of America
by
Sherwin Dodge Printers, Littleton, NH

Cover Photo: *Autumn view from summit cliffs of Mount Willard*, by Robert Kozlow
Map courtesy of State of New Hampshire, Division of Parks and Recreation

Additional copies of this book may be obtained directly from:
Bondcliff Books
P.O. Box 385
Littleton, NH 03561

To Ray Evans,
a 20th century Giant of the Hills

"The sublime and awful grandeur of the Notch baffles all description. Geometry may settle the heights of the mountains, and numerical figures may record the measure; but no words can tell the emotions of the soul, as it looks upward and views the almost perpendicular precipices which line the narrow space between them; while the senses ache with terror and astonishment, as one sees himself hedged in from all the world beside." BENJAMIN WILLEY

TABLE OF CONTENTS

Acknowledgments ix

Introduction xi

1. Geography of Crawford Notch 1

2. Discovery of the Notch and its First Road 7

3. Early Settlers and Lodges 11

4. Willey House Disaster 16

5. Nancy's Romance 22

6. The Railroad Era 25

7. Crawford Notch in the 20th Century 35

8. Hotels of the Crawford Notch Region 41

9. Modern Hospitality Offerings 60

10. Geology of the Notch 62

11. Plants and Wildlife 68

12. White Mountain Weather 81

13. Hiking Guide to Crawford Notch Trails 84

14. Winter Activities in the Notch 117

15. Nomenclature of Crawford Notch 121

16. Bibilography and Historical Sources 142

Acknowledgments

One of the hardest, yet most pleasing aspects of putting together a book such as this is acknowledging all those people who have come forward and offered their knowledge, expertise, and materials during the preproduction stages of this project.

As you will read in the following introduction, my coauthors, John Dickerman and Steve Smith, are the two persons most responsible for getting this book project off the ground in the first place. They have enthusiastically allowed me to significantly alter and expand upon their written efforts of a decade ago, and have offered their thoughts, concerns, and comments on virtually every word and photograph appearing on the following pages. To John and Steve, I owe my heartfelt thanks.

Of course numerous other people have also come forward and offered everything from old photographs and century-old hotel brochures, to hard-to-find historical information, modern day computer technical assistance, and plain old encouragement.

White Mountain National Forest worker Dave Govatski–a walking encyclopedia if I do say so myself–provided invaluable background information on so many aspects of Crawford Notch that it's impossible to list them all here. Having a fellow of his talent and knowledge on my side only made this book that much better. Immeasurable research assistance was also offered by Peter Crane and the staff of the Mount Washington Observatory Resource Center in North Conway; Kathryn Taylor and the marvelous staff of the Littleton Public Library; the staffs of the Lancaster Public Library and the New Hampshire State Library in Concord; Ed Butler, co-owner of the Notchland Inn; historian George Skillwell of Brookline, Massachusetts; and Russ Seybold and the crew of the Conway Scenic Railroad.

Many of the older photographs appearing in this book were loaned to me from private collections. Longtime railroad buff and fellow writer and author Edwin "Bill" Robertson was most generous in allowing me to reproduce a half dozen of his old stereoscopic views. Grand hotel historian Dick Hamilton was also kind enough to provide two old hotel photos, while Arthur "Dick" March of the Littleton Area Historical Society found time to allow me to pore through that organization's huge collection of stereo views. Ultimately, several of the Society's view cards were chosen to appear on these pages. Last but not least, Bob Cook of Titles and Tales bookshop in Littleton loaned me one stereo view from his in-store stock.

Dr. Robert Kozlow must be acknowledged for his major contribution to this project; that being the beautiful photograph from Mount Willard's summit that appears on the cover of this book. There was no shortage of superb photographs to choose from out of Bob's extensive Crawford Notch slide collection. Any one of six or seven of his shots would have sufficed.

The N.H. State Parks Division, and in particular Mary Goodyear, was exceptionally helpful in securing use of the Crawford Notch State Park map for inclusion in this book. Likewise, Tim Leavitt did a superb job in laying this book out on the computer, while Frank Guider and the staff of Foto Factory in Littleton did an incredible job of reprinting most of the old photographs, some of which were of suspect quality to begin with.

Doug Garfield and Sherwin Dodge Printers of Littleton were also a joy to work with in both preparing this book for press and then actually getting it printed for final distribution.

The biggest thanks of all, though, goes to my wife, Jeanne, who encouraged me to pursue this project.

Introduction

To the traveller passing through Crawford Notch by car or train, the natural beauty of this spectacular area of the White Mountains is obvious. Rising high above the Saco River valley both to the east and west are mountains of varying size and shape. From the slide-scarred slopes of Mount Webster to the impressive summit ledges of Mount Willard, Crawford Notch abounds with rugged beauty.

But there is much more to the Notch than its mountainous profile, for it is an area of the White Mountains that is unmatched in natural and human history. From the days of the last ice age, when glaciers carved their way through northern New England, to the early years of the 19th century, when the first permanent settlers took refuge in crude huts and cabins scattered about the immediate region, Crawford Notch has had a storybook existence.

A Guide to Crawford Notch is intended to tell the story of this special area of the White Mountains, both in words and pictures. While many of the legendary stories of the Notch have appeared in numerous publications over the years, this book represents the first attempt we know of to include every aspect of the region's life and times—including its geological, social, and natural history—in one single volume.

The authors of this Crawford Notch compendium like to think this book has something for just about anyone who has ever spent time in the Notch, or is planning to spend time there someday soon. For the naturalist, there are chapters on the geology of the area, its birds and wildlife, and its abundant plant life. For the history buff, there are chapters on the pioneer settlers of the Bretton Woods-Crawford Notch area, the grand hotel era of the late 19th and early 20th centuries, and the legendary stories of the Willey family tragedy and Nancy Barton's fateful trek through the winter wilderness in 1778.

Meanwhile, railroad buffs and riders of the Conway Scenic Railroad excursion trains will find information on the construction of the famous Mountain Division rail line through the Notch a century and a quarter ago, while hiking enthusiasts and mountain explorers will find up-to-date trail information and an accompanying trail map produced by the State of New Hampshire. There's also a section on the nomenclature of the Crawford Notch region, identifying various landmarks and natural features and explaining how or why they received their respective names. There's an extensive bibliography at the end of the book offering readers a list of current and out-of-print publications that can further help satisfy the curiosity of those interested in finding out more about the history of Crawford Notch and the entire White Mountain region. And readers can find out about modern-day Crawford Notch, with information on area lodging and camping facilities in the Bretton Woods-Crawford's area.

The origins of this book date back nearly a decade when John Dickerman and Steve Smith, two longtime hiking buddies who were working in the vicinity of Crawford Notch, compiled a short, brief history of the region. At the time, they intended to self-publish in a small booklet their compilation of facts, figures, and tales of Crawford Notch, but as the years rolled on, their typed 40-page manuscript mainly collected dust as Steve went on to other writing pursuits and John decided to raise a family.

In the spring of 1996, less than a year after the Conway Scenic Railroad began running passenger trains through the Notch and precipitated a resurgence of interest in the area, the idea of finally publishing the decade old manuscript was rekindled when I came across a copy of the original writings while visiting Steve at his Lincoln, N.H. home. This was the only existing copy of the manuscript as John had loaned his out to someone several years earlier, and in the process it was misplaced or lost.

My original intent was to retype the entire manuscript on my computer and make simple revisions as I went along. Once that was done, I'd take a look at the final product and decide (along with John and Steve) if it was worthwhile for publication. My curiosity about the Notch and its legendary past got the best of me shortly after I began revising the document, and before I knew it, I was well on my way toward compiling a much more extensive guide and history to Crawford Notch than any of us had imagined. Soon, the 40-page manuscript had doubled, and then tripled in length. The final version would probably be longer still if I hadn't imposed on myself a strict writing deadline. Certainly there's more interesting information to be found about the Notch and its fascinating history. Perhaps future editions of this book will add even more to the story.

ONE

Geography of the Notch

Crawford Notch is a deep, narrow, glacially carved valley at the southern end of New Hampshire's Presidential Range. The bulk of the Crawford Notch area, situated in the remote mountain hamlet of Hart's Location, is preserved as a state park, while the 773,395-acre White Mountain National Forest encompasses much of the remaining 15 miles of land between the towns of Bartlett and Carroll.

Running roughly in a north-to-south direction, the heart of the Notch is about three miles long and is flanked on both its east and west sides by mountains rising to 3,900 feet above sea level and more. Mount Webster, its west-facing slopes scarred by numerous slides, forms the eastern wall of the Notch. On the opposite side of the Notch, the 4,300-foot peaks of Mount Willey and Mount Field tower some 3,000 feet above the highway, while the smaller, but no less impressive Mount Willard juts out eastward from this higher mountain ridge known as the Willey Range. Willard's steep east slope and Webster's imposing west slope converge at the highest point of the Notch, and it is through the narrow gap or cut between these two mountains that motor vehicle and train traffic is allowed to pass.

The south end of the Crawford Notch area runs nearly to Bartlett and generally follows the course of the Saco River. The mountaintops which rise out of the lower valley on both sides of the Saco are less imposing than those encountered in the Notch proper. The Bemis Ridge peaks of Mount Crawford, Mount Hope and Hart's Ledge bound the river to the east. Mounts Saunders, Bemis, Nancy and the Frankenstein Cliffs guard the lower Notch on its west flank.

A Drive through the Notch

Approach the top of the Notch from Crawford's, an intervale between Mount Tom and the lower slopes of Mount Pierce. The narrow passageway at the north end of the Notch–known as the Gateway– is perhaps the region's most unique feature. "The gateway is as beautiful as it is fantastic," wrote Winthrop Packard in his 1912 book, *White Mountain Trails*. Through this cleft in the mountains–less than 100 feet wide–passes a state highway, a railroad line, and the headwaters of the Saco River.

The term "notch" has been given to mountain defiles throughout the White Mountains due to their striking similarity to that of a notch cut out of a log with an axe. There are more than 20 "notches" scattered across the White Mountains and several more in the vast and wild North Country of northern New Hampshire.

Standing watch over the grand Gateway on its east side is the much photographed Elephant Head profile–a natural rock ledge shaped remarkably like an elephant, complete with an eye and trunk. This prominent landmark is best viewed from Route 302 as it approaches the Notch from the north (or Bretton Woods area).

The elevation of the Gateway stands at just below 1,900 feet, while at the floor of the Notch, near what is known as the Willey House site, the elevation is some 600 feet lower. The distance between the two points is a mere three miles.

The grandeur of Crawford Notch is best on display when one is traveling eastbound along the highway. "The most impressive view...is not gained by riding up through [the Notch] from Bartlett, but by riding down into it," claimed 19th century writer Rev. Thomas Starr King, a true devotee of the White Mountain region.

"The first $^1/_4$ mile is a mere chasm between ruptured cliffs. The remainder is a vast ravine," wrote Rev. Timothy Dwight in his journal on a trip to the region in 1797.

From several viewing points at the top of the Notch, and especially from the summit of Mount Willard, the classic U-shaped cut of the valley shows the work of the glaciers which formed during the last great ice age.

As one proceeds into the notch from its upper end, two roadside waterfalls are passed in just the first half-mile below the Gateway. The impressive Flume Cascade–its name derived from the

The approach to the Gateway of the Notch as seen from Route 302 near the entrance to Crawford Notch State Park.

(PHOTO BY AUTHOR)

narrow trench through which it flows as it nears the highway—is seen first to the left, about 0.4 mile into the descent from the top of the Notch. About 200 yards further is the dramatic Silver Cascade, dropping dramatically down the slopes of Mount Webster. Moses Sweetser, whose early guidebooks to the region lured thousands of visitors to the White Mountains, called the Silver Cascade, "one of the most graceful falls in the mountains. It is the brightest jewel on the route of the railroad." A century ago this waterfall was also commonly known as the "Second Flume."

On the right (west) side of the Notch highway, the cliffs and flumes of Mount Willard (2,865 feet) dominate the upper reaches of the Notch. The Crawford Notch railroad line is seen here winding its way along the base of Willard's precipitous cliffs as it ascends to the Gateway and up to the area known locally as Crawford's. As one proceeds south through the Notch, Willard's mass soon gives way to the steep, scarred slopes of Mount Willey (4,302 feet), which form the western wall of the Notch. Also found on the right and well below the grade of the state highway is dark Dismal Pool, a sizeable but hidden pool of water along the upper Saco River, formed in part by boulders blasted down off Mount Willard during construction of the railroad in the 1870s. Dismal

The slide-scarred slopes of Mount Webster rise steeply above the dam on the Saco River directly across the highway from the Willey House site.

(PHOTO BY AUTHOR)

Pool can be seen from the highway at a point just above the first parking area near the upper cascade. A short trail from this dirt parking area to the pool was cut several years back and is used frequently by fishermen and other visitors.

Three miles south of the Gateway lie Willey Pond and the Willey House site. Willey Pond (also known as Reflection Pond) is a small man-made pond formed by a dam across the Saco River, lying below the great cliffs on the west face of Mount Webster. In summer, stocked trout inhabit the pond, while ducks, moose and many species of birds are also frequent visitors. This area was devastated by a great landslide in 1826, which buried the valley floor in a tumble of trees, dirt, and boulders some 30 feet high and almost a half mile long. The landslide, triggered by a tremendous late summer rainstorm, hurtled down Mount Willey, killing all nine of the settlers who lived in a small house in a clearing on the valley floor. The scars of the slide may still be seen on the slopes of Mount Willey in the form of differing tree growth patterns. The 1826 slide is now completely revegetated.

One mile below the Willey House site (headquarters of Crawford Notch State Park), the Saco River valley swings slightly east as it rounds the southern end of Mount Webster. Here the Appalachian Trail, running some 2,160 miles from Georgia to Maine, crosses the highway and begins its ascent of the southern reaches of the Presidential Range. From this point it's just a two-mile trek north to the ridgeline of the mountain and the stunning Webster Cliffs, and 12.6 miles to the summit of 6,288-foot Mount Washington, the northeast's highest peak.

One of the Crawford Notch area's most scenic natural features, Ripley Falls, is accessed by continuing south on the Appalachian Trail from the road crossing. A half-mile long side trail to the 100-foot high falls on Avalanche Brook is reached a tenth of mile beyond the crossing of the Crawford Notch railroad line.

Below (or south of) the Appalachian Trail, the Saco River valley broadens while the sheer ledges and forested slopes of the Frankenstein Cliffs rise up south and west of the river, standing like a fortress guarding the southern approaches to the Notch.

Just south of the Frankenstein Cliffs, Bemis Brook flows into the Saco from the west, while the Dry River (or Mt. Washington River) flows down from Oakes Gulf and joins the Saco below the state-run Dry River Campground. A mile and a half hike up Bemis Brook leads to Arethusa Falls, at 200 feet, one of the highest waterfalls in the state. These much visited falls are particularly splendid during spring runoff and after a good rainstorm.

As one enters the lower reaches of Crawford Notch, the Saco River runs nearly due south, then bends sharply to the east as it flows through the mountain community of Bartlett, 15 miles south of the Willey House site. The wooded slopes of Mounts Crawford (3,129 feet), Hope (2,520 feet) and Hart's Ledge form the eastern side of the lower Notch, while Mounts Bemis (3,706 feet), Nancy (3,906 feet) and Saunders form the lower western wall.

Nancy Brook, notable for the Nancy Cascades, flows down from Norcross and Nancy Ponds, joining the Saco just below the Notchland Inn, a 19th century English manor several miles south of the state park boundary.

To obtain the best perspectives on Crawford Notch, two hikes are recommended. The 1.6-mile, 45-minute walk up Mount Willard gives one an intimate view of the upper Notch, while the mile-long, 45-minute hike up to the Frankenstein Cliffs affords a good view of the lower Notch.

Mysterious Devil's Den

High up on the south-facing cliffs of Mount Willard—less than 100 feet down from the summit's easternmost ledges—is the Devil's Den, a small cave that appears as a black hole when spied from the highway and the railroad grade, both hundreds of feet below the mountaintop.

The "black-mouthed cavern", as one guidebook writer described it, is about 15 feet high, 20 feet wide and another 20 feet deep. Abel Crawford is credited with finding the cave, while the first person to actually make his way inside the dark mountain cavity—Franklin Leavitt of Lancaster—is supposed to have found scattered bones and skulls littering its floor. Subsequent forays into the cave, including one by Charles Hitchcock's 1870 state survey team, found nothing of the ghastly sort that Leavitt proclaimed spying.

The cave is visited infrequently, and then, only by those who are lowered down to it by ropes. College pranksters have been known on occasion to hang stuffed dummies near or at its entrance. This has resulted in what appears to be a lifeless body dangling from the mountain's sheer south face.

TWO

Discovery of the Notch and its First Road

The discovery of Crawford Notch in 1771 is generally credited to Timothy Nash, a hunter who was tracking a moose on Cherry Mountain, a peak about eight miles west of the Notch. The story goes that he climbed a tree to get his bearings and noticed a break in the rugged mountains before him. Setting off towards this defile, he discovered a rough and rocky, but passable cleft in the mountain wall (now called the 'Gateway of the Notch') through which the headwaters of the Saco River flowed. Nash continued through the pass and proceeded to Portsmouth, where he related his discovery to then Governor Benning Wentworth. The governor, somewhat unsure of Nash's tale, and doubtful that a road could actually be built through the mountain pass, told Nash that if he could bring a horse through the pass and all the way to Portsmouth, he'd grant him a tract of land at the top of the Notch.

Nash returned home, and a few days later with the aid of a friend, one Benjamin Sawyer, set off on the difficult journey. They pushed, pulled, and often lowered the horse on ropes through the pass and down through the length of the Notch, moving rocks, cutting trees, and slowly clearing a rough path through the wilderness. Finally they came to a large boulder with a steep drop-off. They sweated and cursed but eventually managed to lower the horse down the cliff face, at which point they stopped to consume the last of the "spirits" they carried with them for renewed strength. Upon emptying the bottle, Sawyer smashed it against

The Tale of Timothy Nash
— Fact or Fiction?

While the tale of Timothy Nash and his 1771 discovery of the Notch has lived on for more than two centuries, it is doubtful that the legendary North Country hunter was the first "white man" to pass through the mountain pass, as is often reported.

It is generally believed by archaeologists and others who have studied the history of New Hampshire Indians that for years the Native Americans of the region had their own crude path or trail that worked its way through the Notch and over the narrow pass at its north end. Referred to by historians as "The Ammonoosuc Trail," the path began at the upper reaches of the Saco River and passed through the Notch and on to the Ammonoosuc River, which flows westward off the slopes of Mount Washington.

It's probable that Indians living further downstream from the Notch used this path as they made their way to Canada, and at times were no doubt accompanied by captured white men taken from New Hampshire seacoast villages. If that was truly the case, then Nash was not the first white man to set foot through the narrow Gateway of the Notch. Instead, it was some reluctant settler forced into the wilds by his captors.

---

the rock, christening it in his own name. Sawyer Rock still stands today, just west of Route 302, some three miles north of Bartlett village.

From Sawyer's Rock, the path became easier to follow, and in a few days Sawyer and Nash reached Portsmouth with the proof that a passageway had been found through the mountains. True to his word, Gov. Wentworth granted them a tract of land in 1773; land that was named Nash and Sawyer's Location. Their property extended from the top of the Notch to a point just west of what is now Bretton Woods. As a condition of the deal, they were ordered to cut a road through their land to connect with the proposed road through the Notch, and they had to find five families to settle on their land within a five-year period.

The first road was thus laid out through the Notch in the mid and late 1770s. It was a rough, crude passageway that crossed over the Saco River 32 times in its ascent and descent of the Notch. Tradition relates that the first produce carried over this road was a barrel of tobacco taken from Lancaster to Portsmouth in the fall of 1773 by Titus O. Brown, a Lancaster farmer who "raised" the crop on his farm along present day Otter Brook. Conversely, the first cargo to reach Lancaster from the seacoast area was a barrel of rum brought up through the Notch by Capt. Eleazar Rosebrook and several helpers (who supposedly consumed most of the brandy before it arrived safely in the North Country). The rum was offered by a Portland, Maine company to encourage commercial trade through the untamed wilderness of the Notch.

After the Revolutionary War, improvements were effected on the road using funds from a confiscated Tory estate, and in 1803 the road became the Tenth New Hampshire Turnpike. By this time, the "Notch road" was becoming heavily traveled, and a need for places to stay and eat along the route became apparent.

Ethan Allen Crawford's burial plot is found off the Cog Railway Base Road, about a quarter mile from its junction with Route 302 at Fabyan's.
(PHOTO BY AUTHOR)

THREE

Early Settlers and Lodges

Among the earliest settlers of the Notch were Abel and Hannah (Rosebrook) Crawford, who in 1791 bought a tract of land from several other local settlers near what is now Fabyan's (Bretton Woods), and a year later relocated from their home in Guildhall, Vermont with their two children (they eventually had eight sons and a daughter). In January of 1792, Abel's father-in-law, Capt. Eleazar Rosebrook, arrived with his family and purchased Abel's land, whereupon Abel, desirous of plenty of "elbow room" for he and his family, bought another tract 14 miles south in remote Hart's Location.

Abel built a home on his new land and it eventually was developed into the first hotel in Crawford Notch, later gaining the name of the Mount Crawford House. The hotel or inn was in use continuously until it was torn down in the latter part of the 19th century after Dr. Samuel Bemis had taken over Crawford's property by foreclosure just a year after Abel's death.

Abel and his son, Ethan Allen Crawford, are two of the most colorful people in the Notch's history. They became famous as mountain guides, leading many parties of hikers and explorers up the slopes of nearby Mount Washington on the trail they constructed in 1819. The Crawford Path, as this trail is known today, goes from the top of the Notch near Saco Lake, over the peaks of the southern Presidential Range, and on to the 6,288-foot summit of Mount Washington. Its length, from start of finish, is approximately eight miles. The trail was later made into a bridle path by the Crawfords (in 1840), and at the age of 74, Abel Crawford was the first person to make the ascent of Mount Washington on the trail by horse-back. Abel Crawford, known throughout the region as the "Patriarch of the Mountains," died in 1851 at 85 years of age.

Ethan Allen Crawford, appropriately known as the "Giant of the Hills," stood well over six feet tall and is a legendary figure in White Mountain history. Ethan was born in Guildhall, Vt. in 1792 and as an infant moved with his family to the Notch area. Beginning in 1811, Ethan served in the army; a stint that was interrupted for a time when he contracted "spotted fever." At the conclusion of his military service, he worked a variety of jobs and was living in Lou-

Abel Crawford

isville, New York, near where one of his brothers lived, when he learned in a letter that his grandfather (Capt. Rosebrook) was ill with cancer. He returned in 1816 to his grandfather's farm and tavern—opened by Rosebrook in 1803 at Fabyan's Location—intending only to visit for a short time. Instead he was convinced by the dying Rosebrook to stay there permanently. After selling off his land back in New York, Crawford returned for good to Fabyan's, where he soon met and married Lucy Howe, a distant cousin of his. The two of them inherited the Fabyan property upon Rosebrook's death in 1817.

Within a year of his grandfather's passing, however, the tavern burned and Ethan never fully recovered from the loss. For the next six years he worked at several odd jobs, served as a guide for climbing parties, and along with his father built the Crawford Path, the nation's longest continuously maintained hiking trail. It was just a year after the new path was built that Crawford guided a group of Lancaster explorers, plus early 19th century New Hampshire mapmaker Philip Carrigain, to the summit of Mount Washington. It was on this trip that most of the Presidential Range peaks were named.

Crawford later constructed a second route up to Mount Washington. This shorter route up the western slope of the mountain roughly followed the route that the Mount Washington Cog Railway uses today. Crawford is also credited with building (in 1823) the first man-made structures on Washington's summit—three stone huts which provided temporary shelter for hikers. Owing to their crude nature and damp surroundings, however, the huts were apparently little used by the summit's rare visitors.

Between the years 1824 and 1836, Crawford went back into the innkeeping business, constructing a new tavern on the site of his grandfather's original home and farm. Due to poor health and severe financial woes, Crawford chose to "retire" in 1837 and he returned to his birthplace in Guildhall, where he moved to a farm. His retirement from the White Mountains was short-lived, however, as he returned to the area in 1843, renting a rival hotel (which had been built and abandoned) just three-quarters of a mile from his original tavern at Fabyan's.

Ethan and Lucy Crawford lived here until his premature death (from complications related to typhoid fever) on June 22, 1846, at the age of 54. It is not known how Crawford contracted this disease, but quite possibly it was the result of drinking contaminated water. [As late as 1901 and 1902, the town of Littleton, 20 miles west of Crawford Notch, was hit with a typhoid fever epidemic. It's believed that the cause of the outbreak was the tainted waters of the Ammonoosuc River, which flow directly through town and which at that time provided the community with drinking water. As a result of the epidemic, Littleton abandoned the river as a water source and instead constructed a 10-mile pipeline stretching from the side of Mount Garfield in Bethlehem all the way into town.]

Crawford's widow survived until 1869, dying at the age of 66. But it was just after her husband's death in 1846 that she published the first edition of *History of the White Mountains*, the classic book chronicling the Crawford's life in the White Mountains.

As a result of the great works Abel and Ethan performed in and around the Notch, which had originally been called the White Mountain Notch, the pass became known as Crawford Notch to salute these great pioneers.

Another of the early settlements in Crawford Notch was a small house built in 1792 or 1793 by a Mr. Davis, some three miles below the Gateway. This house would later become known

What's in a Presidential Range Name?

Ethan Allen Crawford was more than a pioneer of the region he and his father helped settle some 200 years ago. He was also a pioneer in the annals of White Mountain hiking, for not only did he help construct several early trails to Mount Washington, but he also guided the first women to the mountain's summit (in 1821) and built the first overnight lodging facilities on the summit—three crude stone huts which apparently never caught on with visitors to the mountain.

In the summer of 1820, just a year after he and his father completed work on the Crawford Path to Mount Washington, Ethan Allen Crawford led an expedition to the mountain which resulted in the naming of most of the peaks of the Presidential Range. Known as the Weeks-Brackett party, the group included John W. Weeks, Adino N. Brackett, General John Wilson, Charles J. Stuart, Noyes S. Denison, and Samuel A. Pearson, all of nearby Lancaster, plus Philip Carrigain, the former secretary of state for New Hampshire and publisher of an 1816 map of the state that was considered then to be the most complete in existence.

In the course of their three-day, two-night expedition, the climbers took it upon themselves to choose names for six of the peaks in the mountain range (Mount Washington having been given its name years earlier). Among the Presidential Range summits christened were that of Adams, Jefferson, Madison, Monroe, Franklin and Pleasant. Obviously not all the peaks were named after presidents—there having been just five of them at that point in history. Franklin was named in honor of Benjamin Franklin, famous statesmen, writer, philosopher and scientist of the Revolutionary War era, while Pleasant Mountain was bestowed on the peak we now know as Mount Eisenhower (renamed in honor of Dwight D. Eisenhower, the nation's 34th president). Pleasant Mountain was also known as Dome Mountain at the time of its rechristening. Later references to the peak included the names Pleasant Dome and Mount Prospect.

as the Willey House. A succession of residents lived in it until it was abandoned around 1820. Ethan Allen Crawford reopened it for a short time in 1824, and in 1825, Samuel Willey moved into it with his family and restored it as a house and small inn.

In 1828, the Crawfords built another inn, this one located just above the Gateway, They named it the Notch House. Ethan's brother, Thomas, became manager of this hostel and ran it until around 1850, at which time he was forced to sell the property because of pressing financial obligations. By this time Crawford was also in the process of building a second inn near the Gateway, this one being about a quarter-mile north of the Notch House. The new owners restored the Notch House and completed and opened what would become known as the first Crawford House. Fire, however, claimed both structures within a decade, with the Notch House burning in 1854 and the Crawford House in 1859.

FOUR

Willey House Disaster

"Down came the whole side of the mountain in a cataract of ruin."
Nathaniel Hawthorne – **The Ambitious Guest**, 1835.

Of all the stories and celebrated legends of the White Mountains, the tale of the Willey Slide is perhaps the most tragic. As related in the previous chapter, 38-year-old Samuel Willey moved into the Willey House at the floor of the Notch in the fall of 1825 and reopened it for travelers. With him were his wife, 35-year-old Polly; their five children, Eliza Ann (13), Jeremiah L. (11), Martha Glazier (9), Elbridge Gerry (7), and Sally (5); and two hired hands, David Nickerson (21) and David Allen (37).

In June of the following year, two small rock slides descended from the upper slopes of Mount Willey, which forms the western side of the Notch. The slides gave Willey second thoughts about staying in the Notch, but he opted to keep put with his family as he had already committed much time and effort in establishing a foothold in the rough and rocky valley. He did, however, build an underground shelter a little downstream from the house in case further slides came rumbling down off the side of the mountain.

The summer of 1826 proved exceptionally dry, with no rain for two months. Crops dried up, the Saco River was reduced to a small stream, and the ground was parched to an unusual depth. Finally, on Monday, August 28, the drought ended, but with disastrous results. A tremendous wind and rain storm burst upon the White Mountains and the Notch in particular. By nightfall, the Willeys were stranded, for the rising Saco River had washed out the road.

The historic Willey House, which escaped damage in the tragic 1826 landslide, as it appeared late in the 19th century. The larger structure directly behind the smaller Willey House was built by Horace Fabyan and served as a hotel until its destruction by fire in 1899.
(KILBURN STEREO COURTESY BILL ROBERTSON)

By dawn of the next day, the Saco had risen an incredible 24 feet, flooding the river valley all the way south to Conway. The storm had finally abated, but great destruction had been wrought in Crawford Notch. Dozens of landslides had denuded the hill-sides; crops, houses, and livestock had been washed downstream; 21 of the 32 bridges along the highway had been washed out.

The first person to reach the Willey House after the storm was a Mr. John Barker, who had descended through the Notch from Ethan Allen Crawford's inn. When he reached the Willey House late in the day on Tuesday, the debris of a great landslide lay all about the house, but the homestead itself was untouched, having been spared destruction by a ridge of boulders behind the house which had split the slide in two as it roared down the slopes of Mount Willey. Barker looked but could find no trace of Samuel Willey or his family. He did come across the family dog, and the following morning, an ox, pinned under the remains of a flattened stable just a few yards from the main house.

Assuming the Willeys had fled from their home to Abel Crawford's place, a few miles further south, Barker resumed his journey. Arriving at Crawford's, Barker related his findings and soon learned that no sign or word from the Willeys had been heard since the terrible storm had struck. A rescue party was then organized, and the group struck off for the Willey place on Thursday. Sadly, the rescuers discovered the partially buried bodies of Mr. and Mrs. Willey, the two hired men, and two of the Willey children. The three other Willey youths were never found, evidently buried beneath the great mass of boulders, dirt, and trees which had come crashing down off the mountain.

What actually happened to the Willeys will never be known, but two widely accepted theories are that the family, fearing the rising waters of the Saco, had fled to higher ground, only to be caught on the mountain when the slide occurred; or that the family fled to their underground shelter, but were overwhelmed before they could even reach it.

The deadly slide itself stretched over half a mile down the side of Mount Willey, denuding a great portion of the mountain and depositing piles of debris around the Willey House up to 30 feet deep, but leaving the little home unscathed. The slide was heard as far away as Whitefield, some 20 miles northwest of the Notch.

The storm also did great damage to other areas in and around the Notch. Down at Abel Crawford's tavern six miles south of the Willey House, the raging Saco River overflowed its banks, ruining much of the elder Crawford's farmland. A new sawmill, just built by Crawford, was swept away, along with logs and fence posts encircling the farm.

In his book, *The White Hills*, written in 1859, author Thomas Starr King wrote of the elder Crawford's dilemma, "Mr. Crawford was not at home; but the heroic wife placed lighted candles in the windows, and to prevent the house from being demolished by the jam that was threatening it, stood at a window near the corner, and in the midst of the tempest, pushed away with a pole the

A memorial tablet marking the site of the historic Willey House is shown here shortly after it was placed in the Notch in 1925 by the Anna Stickney Chapter of the Daughters of the American Revolution. The tablet is found today at the State Park headquarters across from Willey Pond.
(PHOTO COURTESY CRAWFORD NOTCH STATE PARK)

timber, which the mad current would send as a bettering ram against the wall."

The storm, of course, also did tremendous damage to the road and bridges through the Notch, but with their typical industrious spirit, the Crawfords soon began the work of rebuilding the highway through the mountain pass.

The recovered bodies of the landslide victims were first buried next to the Willey House, but were later removed to a cemetery at Intervale, just outside North Conway village. The small burial plot where the Willeys were laid to rest can be found behind the Scottish Lion on Route 302 and 16, a short distance past the scenic overlook west of North Conway. The body of David Allen, one of the Willey's hired hands, is buried in a cemetery in nearby Bartlett.

The Willey House lay vacant for just a year as a Mr. Pendexter reopened it as an inn in the fall of 1827. For the next 17 years the house went through a succession of innkeepers until Horace Fabyan acquired it in 1844. Fabyan repaired the Willey House and built a two and a half story inn adjacent to it. This remained in operation until fire destroyed both buildings on Sept. 24, 1899.

The Willey tragedy, which has been told in print many times over in the last one and a half centuries, was the basis for 19th century novelist Nathaniel Hawthorne's classic short story, *The Ambitious Guest.* Hawthorne (1804-1864) penned the tale after a visit to the Notch area in 1832.

Natural Disasters of the Notch

The killer 1826 landslide in Crawford Notch has gone down in history as the greatest natural disaster ever to take place in this wild and rugged section of the White Mountains. But Crawford Notch has not been immune to natural disasters in the 170 years since the famous Willey Slide occurred.

On Sept. 21, 1938, the Crawford Notch area and the entire White Mountain region were blasted by the greatest hurricane to strike New England in this century. Chief among the hurricane's victims, at least in the Notch area, were two stands of virgin softwood timber—one on the east side of the height-of-land between Mounts Field and Tom, the other in the watershed of Nancy Brook on the eastern slopes of Mount Nancy. The Nancy Brook timber stand contained several million board feet of virgin timber.

The hurricane also took its toll on area hiking trails, including the just completed Nancy Pond Trail along Nancy Brook. It would be another 22 years before this mountain trail was open to trampers again. The popular carriage road to Mount Willard, long a favorite of Crawford House guests, was hit hard by the storm as well. The hurricane, in fact, pretty much laid to waste recent efforts by Civilian Conservation Corps (CCC) workers who had reconstructed and relocated sections of the road to make it passable for automobiles. Meanwhile, at the base of Mount Willard, the historic Crawford House temporarily lost its water supply when a windblown tree fell across its main supply line.

Twenty-one years later, in October 1959, following a period of heavy rains, the state-run wildlife preserve at the base of Mount Webster (across from the Willey House site) was threatened when a landslide came down off the face of the mountain. "The roar was dreadful," wrote state park manager Donald Mitchell in an account of the slide in the June 1961 edition of *Appalachia*. Mitchell said the moving mass of rocks and trees was 70 to 150 feet wide at the front and cut a swath to a depth of 15-20 feet. Fearing both floodwaters and the consequences of the landslide, he was able to lug many of the preserve's animals to safety, going so far as to put a bear under the park manager's cabin and a skunk in one of the park's sheds.

Even as recently as the fall of 1995 and the winter of 1995-96, several heavy rainstorms caused considerable flood damage in the Notch, especially near the Willey House site, where culverts were plugged by debris and runoff from the slopes of Mount Willey poured across state park grounds and Route 302. The railroad grade through the Notch and south toward Bartlett sustained heavy damage as well, forcing the Conway Scenic Railroad to delay running trains on the old Mountain Division line until late June of 1996.

FIVE

Nancy's Romance

In 1778, when the road through Crawford Notch was little more than a rough footpath, a sad tale of deceit and death occurred in the Notch.

A young woman from Jefferson, Nancy Barton, was living and working on Col. Joseph Whipple's farm when she became engaged to a farmhand. Wedding preparations were begun, the marriage to take place in Portsmouth in December of that year. One day, shortly before the young couple were to leave for the seacoast, Nancy, having entrusted her lover with the money she had painstakingly saved for two years, went to Lancaster for some last minute preparations for their trip. Upon returning to the Whipple farm, she discovered her fiancee was gone, along with all her money.

Stricken by grief, Nancy resolved to follow her husband-to-be, hoping she might catch him encamped in the vicinity of the Notch. Despite strong protestations from her co-workers and landlord, she set off in the cold and snow that had suddenly befallen the region.

Nancy Barton made the difficult 20-mile journey to the top of the Notch on foot, traveling all night through the storm and bitter cold. When she arrived at her fiancee's campsite, she discovered he had already fled, the ashes from his fire as cold as the December air.

Undeterred, Nancy began the descent of the Notch, through deep snow and over icy rocks and streams. At last, utterly exhausted, she collapsed in the snow on the banks of a stream some nine miles from the top of the Notch. Here she was found frozen to death a few hours later, by a search party sent out by Col. Whipple.

Nancy's unfaithful lover, hearing of the tragedy that befell her, became insane and died shortly afterwards, stricken with remorse over the consequences of his action. According to local legend, his agonized wailings can be heard in the wind on cold, dark December nights.

The brook by which she died became known as Nancy Brook, while a nearby mountain was named Mount Nancy, in memory of the spurned Nancy Barton.

SIX

The Railroad Era

In the winter of 1867, a group of Maine businessmen, including a former state governor, formed the Portland and Ogdensburg Railroad Company. Their purpose was to build a rail line from Portland, Maine to Ogdensburg, New York through the White Mountains, by which they hoped to take part in the ever increasing commercial trade with the west, and specifically the Great Lakes region. Although their plans to build the railroad all the way to Ogdensburg—a town on the St. Lawrence River northeast of Lake Ontario—never materialized, what they did manage to accomplish had a tremendous impact on Crawford Notch and the White Mountains.

The Portland and Ogdensburg Railroad was granted a charter by the Maine legislature on Feb. 11, 1867. The charter authorized the company to build a rail line from Portland west to the New Hampshire state line, where it would connect there with a proposed railroad line that would cut across the Granite State to the eastern boundary of Vermont. At about the same time, a group of New Hampshire businessmen successfully petitioned their home state to form the Portland, White Mountains and Ogdensburg Railroad. The New Hampshire group never got its financial act together, however, and its charter was eventually surrendered to the Portland and Ogdensburg Railroad in 1869.

OPPOSITE PAGE: *Construction crew members work on building the railroad line through the Gateway at the top of the Notch. Behind them is seen the Crawford House hotel.*
(PHOTO COURTESY CRAWFORD NOTCH STATE PARK)

In July of 1867, the corporators of the P and O met and hired two Portland engineers to make a preliminary survey of the proposed railroad through Maine and New Hampshire. The engineers, John F. Anderson and Charles J. Noyes, offered a preliminary report to P and O officials in May 1868 and recommended a route that would bring the line from Portland to Conway, and then through the heart of the White Mountains and rugged Crawford Notch. They estimated it would cost $3 million to construct the new railroad.

The following year was a big one for the P and O. In January, the railroad company was formally organized and Samuel J. Anderson, brother of John Anderson, was elected president. Six months later, on July 7, 1869, the New Hampshire legislature authorized the P and O to extend its railroad line through the state, but only under the condition that it not pass around or run outside of Crawford Notch. The railroad company was also required to spend $100,000 in New Hampshire before July 1, 1873, and have the entire line completed by January 1, 1880.

Just two years after the first spike for the new railroad had been unceremoniously driven into the ground on Aug. 6, 1869 (in Portland), trains were running regularly from Portland to North Conway, and within four more years the P and O had completed a great engineering marvel, having built the rail line up through wild and rugged Crawford Notch and all the way to Fabyan's.

Preliminary construction of the railroad through Crawford Notch began in 1874, and by August of that year the line reached as far as the Mount Crawford House. By the end of the 1874 construction season, rails had been laid as far as the Frankenstein Cliffs, some nine miles distant from Bartlett, while work had also begun on the upper reaches of the Notch. Completion of the line all the way through the Notch was celebrated August 7, 1875, with the final spike being driven into a railroad tie near the "Great Cut." Regular passenger service between Portland and Fabyan's commenced two days later, with round trip fares advertised at $2.75 a ticket. The P and O line was also completed all the way to Johnson, Vt. by year's end. The total distance between Portland and Johnson was 193 miles.

Constructing such a railroad through the rugged Notch was truly a remarkable achievement, for the line was built right into the sides of the mountains, with the rise in altitude from North Conway to Crawford's (at the top of the Notch) being 1369 feet

*The eastbound Portland and Ogdensburg Railroad Engine No. 11 passes
over Frankenstein Trestle on its way through the Notch toward Bartlett.*
(KILBURN BROTHERS STEREO COURTESY BILL ROBERTSON)

in the nearly 26-mile long section. From Bemis House at the south
end of the Notch to the Crawford House (just past the Gateway),
the grade has an average rise of 116 feet per mile.

Two notable achievements of the railroad builders were the
great train trestles constructed 4.1 miles apart in the Notch. The
lower of the two, the Frankenstein Trestle, is about 500 feet long
and 80 feet high and was completed in June 1875. The original
trestle was "rebuilt" (and strengthened) in 1895 by adding additional support. In essence, a stronger trestle was built around the
existing structure, creating a bridge within a bridge. This was done
so that the trestle could accommodate heavier locomotives and
trains. The trestle was named in honor of Godfrey Frankenstein,

A locomotive heading east through the Notch passes by the Mount Willard Section Dwelling and over Willey Brook Bridge.
(KILBURN BROTHERS STEREO COURTESY BILL ROBERTSON)

an artist of German birth who painted nearby White Mountain scenes in the 19th century.

The second great railroad span was the Willey Brook Bridge, built over the deep gulf above Willey Brook near the top of the Notch. This trestle, also completed early in the summer of 1875, is 140 feet long and extends across a ravine some 90 feet deep. Interestingly, the north end of this trestle was originally of wooden construction, while the south end was made of iron. The entire span was reconstructed in 1905, with iron girders replacing the inferior wood structure.

Another major feat accomplished by the railroad construction crew was the cutting of a passageway through the narrow Gateway at the top of the Notch. To accomplish this, workers had to blast their way through the ledge on the west side of the Gate-

A wood-fired locomotive advances through the narrow Gateway of the Notch. Notice the crude, dirt roadway just to the right of the train tracks, and the platform or roof over the tracks. It's believed the platform was used to protect passing trains from rock slides and snow slides.

(KILBURN STEREO COURTESY BILL ROBERTSON)

way, then haul the rock debris away to allow for construction of the permanent railway bed.

All things considered, the railroad work through the Notch took a remarkably short time, considering that human and animal labor were responsible for moving the tons of rock and dirt necessary to create the smooth, level ledge on which the tracks sit. Along with the line itself were also built four trackside houses for section bosses and their families to live in. Perhaps the most famous of these was the Mount Willard Section Dwelling, built alongside the tracks at the north end of Willey Brook Bridge. This house and some of its longtime occupants—the Loring Evans family—are immortalized in the 1983 book, *Life by the tracks*, by Virginia C. Downs. All that remains today of this truly isolated structure is its foundation.

The builders of the railroad through the Notch—including P and O president Samuel J. Anderson (1824-1905) and the railroad chief engineer, John F. Anderson (1823-1887)—are memorialized with a roadside monument situated off Route 302 about a half-mile from the entrance to the Mount Washington Hotel in Bretton Woods. The bronze tablet recognizing their efforts is found off the south side of the highway, almost opposite the Stickney Memorial Chapel

The Portland and Ogdensburg Railroad, which ran into serious financial problems in the mid-1880s, was eventually forced in January 1887 to turn over its entire rail operation—including the line through the Notch—to the newly-formed Portland and Ogdensburg Railway. Just a year and a half later, the line was leased to the Maine Central Railroad (for a term of 999 years), and it was renamed the Mountain Division line. Maine Central retained ownership of the rail line through Crawford Notch up until just a few years ago (1994).

The impact of the railroad through the Notch had a far reaching effect in the latter years of the 19th century and the early years of the following century. Thanks to the railroad, the mountains were now readily accessible to everyone, and the comfort of a scenic train ride, rather than the rough and tumble stage or carriage trip, brought many new visitors to the region, and spurred the steadily increasing hotel and tourist trades to new heights. At the same time, the railroad paved the way for the lumber barons' intrusion into the mountains, and the great devastation they would wreak in the years just before and after the turn of the century.

A Conway Scenic Railroad train crosses Frankenstein Trestle on its way from North Conway village to Bretton Woods.

(PHOTO BY AUTHOR)

But passenger trains gradually lost favor with White Mountain visitors as roads improved and automobile travel became the norm. With ridership dwindling, passenger trains ceased running through the Notch in the late 1950s, with daily service between Portland and St. Johnsbury ending on April 26, 1958. The owners of the historic Crawford House, along with several other area businessmen, did for a time consider operating a summer tourist train (with a vintage steam locomotive) through the Notch, but their plans fell through in 1971 when it became apparent that insurance costs would be prohibitive. Regularly scheduled freight service through the Notch was next to disappear, with the last planned run taking place on September 3, 1983. A few unscheduled transport runs did occur over the next year or so, with the last trains passing along the Mountain Division in the fall of 1984.

For a decade the Notch rail line sat empty. Weeds and trees began sprouting up in between the railroad ties. Miniature landslides fell across the tracks too, blocking the way even if a train had wanted to made the trek through the mountains. The State of New Hampshire, anxious to restore some type of rail service through the Notch, stepped into the picture in 1994 and purchased the Mountain Division line from Guilford Transportation, owners of the Maine Central Railroad. The state then offered to lease the line to prospective entrepreneurs wishing to run tourist trains along its rails. The Conway Scenic Railroad, based in nearby North Conway, was awarded a five-year lease (with an option for five additional years) in the summer of 1994. After extensive rehabilitation work was undertaken that fall and through the spring and summer of the following year, passenger rail service was finally restored to the former Mountain Division line in September 1995. On Sept. 1, the Conway Scenic Railroad ran its first excursion train from North Conway to Crawford's. By the end of the 1996 summer season, the popular daily excursion trains were rolling an additional four miles to Fabyan's and Bretton Woods. Within a few more years, the line may be restored all the way to Whitefield.

A Conway Scenic Railroad train pulls into Fabyan's Station during a fall 1996 excursion.   (PHOTO BY AUTHOR)

Conway Scenic Railroad

Twenty-one years after returning passenger train service to the tourist hub of North Conway, the Conway Scenic Railroad did the same to historic Crawford Notch in the fall of 1995, when it began running daily excursion trains from North Conway to Crawford's.

The Conway Scenic Railroad was founded in May 1974 by several local businessmen and Dwight Smith of Portland, Maine, a Boston and Maine Railroad worker and devoted railfan. It was Smith, while on a 1968 excursion trip to North Conway, who first dreamed up the idea of converting the abandoned train depot and rail yard there into an operating rail museum with vintage steam trains and a reactivated train depot.

After running into several roadblocks—including a court battle over rights to the tracks then owned by the B and M— the CSRR went operational on August 4, 1974, selling 93 tickets on its first 11-mile round-trip run between North Conway and Conway villages.

Over time, the tourist train line grew into one of the region's most popular attractions. Refurbished steam engines and diesel locomotives were added to its growing fleet, as were restored passenger coaches. The railroad's operating season also expanded as special holiday-related trains were added to the summer and fall schedule.

Smith, who served as president and general manager of the railroad until his retirement in 1990, was succeeded in the dual posts by Russ Seybold. It was under Seybold's leadership that the CSRR was awarded (on September 1, 1994) a five-year lease to operate a tourist train line from its North Conway headquarters up through Crawford Notch.

After obtaining the lease from the state, CSRR crews began chipping and cutting away at a decade's worth of growth along the former Mountain Division line between Intervale and Crawford's. On December 17, 1994, the inaugural run from North Conway to Bartlett was made. Less than nine months later, train service was restored all the way through the Notch to Crawford's, with a "Directors Special" making the first trip on August 26, 1995 and the inaugural passenger run being made a week later on September 1.

Despite damaging fall and winter storms in late 1995 and early 1996—which resulted in numerous washouts and the loss of one bridge—CSRR began its first full season of excursion train runs on June 22, 1996. By September 1, trains were running regularly to Fabyan's, and in late October, one train, carrying members of the 470 Railroad Club of Portland, made it nearly into Twin Mountain, running almost four miles past the usual terminus point of the Crawford Notch runs.

SEVEN

Crawford Notch in the 20th Century

In the first decade of this century, there was much concern in New Hampshire over the wholesale destruction being done to the White Mountains by extensive logging operations. The devastation wrought by the lumberjacks' axes and saws was bad enough. To top that off, forest fires, fueled by the slash left from the cutting of great sections of woodland, often raged for days, laying to waste even larger tracts of once pristine forest land.

In 1911, the New Hampshire legislature passed a bill allowing the state to purchase Crawford Notch and thus save the area from further damage. Through a failure to provide sufficient funds, however, the state was not able to buy the entire Notch area, but in 1913 the state acquired the upper six miles of Crawford Notch. That 5,975 acre tract was bought for $62,000.

The Crawford Notch land purchase was inspired by passage in 1911 of the Weeks Act, a federal bill through which the government began to purchase large tracts of eastern wilderness lands to be set aside as national preserves. One of the first purchases was 30,000 acres in the White Mountains, which became the first federally-owned land in the new White Mountain National Forest. Today, the WMNF encompasses more than 773,395 acres in both north-central New Hampshire and extreme western Maine.

In 1922, nine years after the state purchase of the Crawford Notch land, the Willey House clearing in the heart of the Notch was leased to two Bartlett men—Donahue and Hamlin—who built log cabins, a restaurant and gift shop, and cleared viewpoints for

The popular Willey House Camps attracted motorists to Crawford Notch in the early part of the 20th century. While most of the buildings from that era no longer exist, the larger log structures pictured above still stand and today serve as the gift shop and snack bar at the Willey House site in Crawford Notch State Park.

(POSTCARD COURTESY CRAWFORD NOTCH STATE PARK)

better access to the mountain vistas in the immediate area. A visit to the present day Crawford Notch State Park Information and Interpretive Center shows many old photographs and postcards from this era.

Eventually the small log cabins were removed, to be replaced by picnic areas and scenic roadside parking areas. A dam was also constructed across from the Willey House site so that a pond could be created. The original dam was replaced by the state in the early 1970s. For many summers the state also operated a wildlife exhibit just across the dam at the foot of Mount Webster. Many of New Hampshire's native animals were featured in the exhibit.

Crawford Notch State Park was created in 1950, with the state managing the park, the wildlife exhibit and a new campground

---

OPPOSITE PAGE: *The Willey House site and Willey Pond as they appeared nearly a half century ago.*

(AUTHOR'S COLLECTION)

built near the southern entrance to the park. The gift shop and restaurant were also reopened, and quickly the park became one of the most visited and popular in the entire state park system.

In the years since there have been changes–but few major ones–in Crawford Notch State Park. The wildlife exhibit was removed in 1973, and an extensive development plan for the state park was prepared, but never implemented, due to lack of funds. A few of the old cabins and buildings from the Donahue-Hamlin era are still in use by the state. These structures house the present day snack bar and gift shop and the Information and Interpretive Center.

The Notch has managed to retain its wild, undeveloped character, even though thousands of tourists visit it each year. The pond and dam across from the Willey House clearing, in fact, provided the dramatic setting for scenes in the 1993 feature length film, *Where the Rivers Flow North*, starring Rip Torn, Tantoo Cardinal and Michael J. Fox.

One reason for Crawford Notch's enduring popularity is its many walking trails, which offer hiking opportunities to trampers of all ages and abilities. These include easy paths through the woods and along the Saco River. Others are more strenuous and ascend to the high peaks of the region, including several southern neighbors of Mount Washington, highest of all the great White Mountain summits.

"Where the Rivers Flow North"

Hollywood, or at least northern New England's version of Tinseltown, came to the Crawford Notch area in late 1992 when Willey Pond and its dam across the Saco River were the setting for several key scenes in the full-length motion picture, "Where the Rivers Flow North," starring Rip Torn, Tantoo Cardinal, Michael J. Fox, and Treat Williams.

The Kingdom County Productions film, based on a novella by northern Vermont writer Howard Frank Mosher, told the story of an old-time logger and his longtime live-in Native American companion, who try to prevent the construction of a new power dam that, if built, will flood the logger's land. The climactic scene of the picture, in which Noel Lord (played by Torn) attempts to "drive" logs down the river, utilized Willey

Actress Tantoo Cardinal, left, and actor Rip Torn, right, play out a scene during the 1992 filming of Where the Rivers Flow North. *In this particular scene, the setting is the dam across the Saco River in Crawford Notch State Park.*

(PHOTO BY AUTHOR)

Pond and the Saco River dam, which was completely rebuilt for the movie so as to resemble a dam from 1927, which is the year in which the story takes place.

Despite below-freezing temperatures and occasional snow flurries, production crews were able to film the Willey Pond scenes over a long weekend period in mid-November 1992. Portions of the critically acclaimed film, released the following year, were also shot in nearby Bethlehem.

EIGHT

Hotels of the Crawford Notch Region

The hotels, taverns and inns of the Crawford Notch area have played a large role in the history and development of the region. From the 1820s to the 1920s, many politicians, scientists, philosophers, businessmen and adventurers frequented the inns and hotels of the area, using them as bases from which they could climb and explore the mountains, or gather geological, meteorological and botanical samples and information for scientific study.

The following is a brief compilation of the hotels and inns of Crawford Notch. Some were simple rustic inns, others were among the grandest, most luxurious hotels of the Gilded Age. All but two are gone now, most the victims of fires and changing times.

Mount Crawford House

One of the earliest and most important inns was the Mount Crawford House, built by Abel Crawford sometime around 1800 on his property some nine miles south of the Gateway, near the present day location of the Notchland Inn. Abel and his sons eventually constructed a 30-room tavern and inn which became popular and famous for its good food and accommodations. Among the most notable guests were Daniel Webster and President Franklin Pierce. The building suffered some damage in the

OPPOSITE PAGE: *The grand Crawford House hotel as seen from the eastern shore of Saco Lake, headwaters of the Saco River.*
(AUTHOR'S COLLECTION)

great flood of August 1826, but stayed in operation until after Abel Crawford's death in 1851.

Dr. Samuel A. Bemis took ownership of the tavern and Crawford's 250-acre farm shortly thereafter, foreclosing on the property which was by then under the management of Nathaniel T.P. Davis, Crawford's son-in-law. Bemis, a retired Boston dentist who made his fortune manufacturing dentures, used the inn as his home while building a grand stone villa (today's Notchland Inn) on the same property. Railroad construction crews reportedly lived in the aging building during the time the Crawford Notch rail line was being built, and reputedly left the place in shambles and apparently uninhabitable. Following Dr. Bemis' death in 1880, and several years after the old Crawford tavern had been permanently closed to the public, the building was torn down, its best days by then far removed.

Old Moosehorn Tavern and the Mount Washington House

North of the Notch, in the vicinity of the "Giant's Grave" (a large glacially deposited mound) near present-day Bretton Woods, a number of hostelries were built throughout the 19th century. The first of these was Capt. Eleazar Rosebrook's inn, a two-story tavern built in 1803 after Rosebrook had resettled in the area from Guildhall, Vermont in 1792. Captain Rosebrook died in 1817, and his grandson, Ethan Allen Crawford, inherited the inn, but the building accidentally burned to the ground just a year after Crawford took ownership when a candle left burning in a kitchen chair touched off a disastrous fire.

In 1824, Ethan began enlarging the small house that had replaced the Rosebrook inn, and this structure became known as The Old Moosehorn Tavern. Ethan added more rooms in 1832-1833, but beset by financial problems, he sold the property to Horace Fabyan of Portland, Maine in 1837. Mr. Fabyan undertook significant renovations to the building over the next decade, going so far as to add a three-story addition to the structure for the opening of the 1848 summer season. One tourist guidebook of the era called the inn the "most famous" of the region. Like so many of the other great hotels of the area, however, the building, by then known as the Mount Washington House, succumbed to fire in the spring of 1853. The hotel's stables, which were spared in the 1853 blaze, were destroyed five years later after being struck by lightning.

Guests gather on the porch of the White Mountain House in this photo taken around 1871.
(KILBURN BROTHERS STEREO VIEW COURTESY DICK HAMILTON)

White Mountain House

Sometime around 1831, the White Mountain House was opened about three-quarters of a mile west of the "Giant's Grave," in an area just about opposite that of the present-day Above the Notch Motor Inn. At first a small inn, operated by William Dennison of Jefferson, a rival neighbor of Ethan Allen Crawford's, it was eventually purchased by the Rosebrooks and enlarged in the early 1840s. Later it was occupied and operated by Ethan and Lucy Crawford for a few years until his death in 1846.

The White Mountain House was refurbished and refurnished around 1850 by its new owner, a Col. John H. White, and it thrived in the 1850s and 1860s, being the only inn above the Notch from 1853 (when the Mount Washington House burned) to 1872, when the luxurious Fabyan House was built. Among its most prominent guests were President Ulysses S. Grant and Edward, Prince of Wales (and later King of England).

The White Mountain House continued in operation well into the 20th century, with its last owners being Mrs. Margaret Sheehe, and her daughter Mary and son Joseph Alfred Seymour, who bought the hotel in 1907. Just a few years after a new dining room and additional sleeping rooms were constructed, the four-story

hotel was victimized by a nighttime fire a short while after it had closed for the season. The October 8, 1929 blaze, which began near the roof, leveled the building in just two hours. All that firefighters were able to save were a small section of the kitchen, a nearby cottage, a barn, and several other outbuildings. All hotel records, including its old registers, were lost in the fire that newspapers accounts of the day reported cost the owners $100,000 in losses.

Fabyan House

In 1873, the Mount Washington Hotel Company opened the 200-room Fabyan House near the former site of the Mount Washington House. The hotel was named for Horace Fabyan, the Portland, Maine businessman who operated the original hotel at the site in the years prior to its destruction by fire. Among the investors in the Fabyan House venture was Sylvester Marsh (1803-1884), the creative and inventive mind behind the building of the Cog Railway up Mount Washington.

With the opening of the Portland and Ogdensburg Railroad line through the Notch in 1875, Fabyan's—as the locality was known—became one of the busiest centers in the mountains, and would remain so for many years to come. John Lindsay and a Mr. French operated the Fabyan House for five years, then leased the operation to Asa Barron, who was one of three principals in the famous area hotel operating company, Barron, Merrill, and Barron. In the company's heyday, it operated four hotels in the region—the Fabyan House, Twin Mountain House, Crawford House, and the Summit House atop Mount Washington.

Col. Oscar G. Barron (1850-1913), Asa's son, managed the Fabyan House for some 35 years beginning in 1878. Along with his expertise in hotel management, Barron carried some political clout as he successfully advocated—along with several regional and state conservation organizations—state purchase of land in Crawford Notch in the early part of this century. After his death at the age of 62, his widow, Jennie Barron, managed the Fabyan House for another 17 years.

OPPOSITE PAGE: *A passenger train and locomotive rest on the tracks in front of the historic Fabyan House hotel at Bretton Woods.*
(KILBURN BROTHERS STEREO VIEW COURTESY BOB COOK)

Moses Sweetser, writing in the 1887 edition of the popular *Chisholm's White Mountain Guide-Book*, said of the hotel, "The external architecture...is of the simplest order, but the rooms within

---

The Curse of the Giant's Grave

A large glacially-deposited mound of earth—described in various accounts as being anywhere from 30 to 60 feet high—was home to several of the early dwellings and inns around Fabyan's. It was on this mound, called the "Giant's Grave," that Capt. Eleazar Rosebrook built the first inn for travelers in the Crawford Notch-Bretton Woods area. The two-story dwelling on the west end of the Giant's Grave featured two underground rooms and "from the chamber in the second story, was an outside door, which opened so that one could walk out on the hill, which was beautiful, and gave a view of all the flat country around it," recalled Ethan Allen Crawford in the Crawford family's epic memoir, *History of the White Mountains.*

After fire destroyed the White Mountain House, the second lodging establishment to be built at the Giant's Grave, the mound was permanently removed—much to the consternation of many—during construction of the Fabyan House hotel.

One old White Mountain legend, related by John G. Spaulding in his 1855 book *Historical Relics of the White Mountains,* tells of an Indian, "Who many years ago, stood on that mound, with a blazing pitch-pine torch, lighted at a tree struck by lightning, and swinging it wildly around in the darkness, he said, 'No pale-face shall take deep root here; this the Great Spirit whispered in my ear.'"

As history well documents, all three buildings constructed at the Giant's Grave eventually fell victim to fires, with the Fabyan House the last to be destroyed in 1951. Even the annex to the Fabyan House, which was used mainly as a residence for hotel workers, succumbed to fire on May 26, 1967. Coincidence or not, the fates of these buildings have done nothing to dispel the myth of the Giant's Grave.

are high-studded and airy, and the halls wide and commodious."
According to hotel advertisements of the day, it could accommodate up to 500 guests and daily rates were $4.50.

The four-story Fabyan House operated successfully for many
years, but in the early morning hours of Sept. 19, 1951, the famed
landmark "was reduced to ashes in less than an hour" reported
local newspapers after fire swept through the building just 10 days
after the closing of the hotel's summer and fall season..

*Guests of the Mount Pleasant House at Bretton Woods arrive by horse
and carriage.*
(PHOTO COURTESY LITTLETON AREA HISTORICAL SOCIETY)

Mount Pleasant House

The Mount Pleasant House, located about one mile east of the
Fabyan House, was built in 1876 by John Leavitt, who then sold
the property to Oscar Pittman and Joseph Stickney in 1881. Stickney
became sole owner in 1895 and is generally credited with creating
a beautiful resort hotel which for a time was known as the "flag-
ship" of the grand hotels managed by the Barron hotel group.
Abbott L. Fabyan, son of Horace Fabyan, managed the hotel for
the Barrons for about a decade in the 1880s and 1890s.

The Mount Pleasant House had 150 rooms, and commanded

one of the finest views of the Presidential Range from its trackside terrace overlooking the fields and forests of the winding Ammonoosuc River valley. It received its name from a mountain peak of the same name. That mountain today is known as Mount Eisenhower–the round, bald 4,761-foot peak a few miles south of Mount Washington.

Under Stickney's ownership, the original hotel building was basically rebuilt, and as historian Frederick W. Kilbourne wrote in 1916, "it was transformed into virtually a new establishment...which achieved a high reputation." After Stickney and his widow died–he in 1903, she in 1932–the hotel's last owner, her nephew, decided the establishment was not profitable and the building was torn down in 1939. Today, the site of the Mount Pleasant House is home to the modern Bretton Woods Motor Inn, which still retains one of the finest views in the region of Mount Washington and its neighboring peaks.

Mount Washington Hotel

Joseph Stickney wanted to own the most elegant hotel in the mountains, and in 1901 he began construction on a new hotel on a small rise three-quarters of a mile north of the Mount Pleasant House. The hotel was designed by New York architect Charles Alling Gifford and the style is of the Spanish Renaissance. A foundation of granite and a superstructure of wood was laid on a steel frame, and the largest wooden structure in New England, the Mount Washington Hotel, opened for business on July 28, 1902 with a ball and banquet attended by, among others, several descendants of the famous Crawford family. Equipped with its own golf course, miles of riding and walking trails, large stables, and housing for hundreds of employees, the Mount Washington Hotel was a small city in itself. Situated on a knoll with tremendous views of the surrounding mountains and Crawford Notch, the hotel quickly became popular with the New York and Boston socialites of the era.

OPPOSITE PAGE: *Joseph Stickney's remodeled Mount Pleasant House occupied the spot where the modern day Bretton Woods Motor Lodge now stands.*

(PHOTO COURTESY DICK HAMILTON)

Stickney did not long enjoy his palatial new hotel, however, as he died on Dec. 31, 1903, barely a year and a half after the grand structure first opened. His wife, Carolyn, in later years known as the "Princess" because of her subsequent marriage to a European prince, owned and operated the resort for close to 30 more years until her death in 1932.

The Mount Washington Hotel's fortunes declined during the Depression and World War II years, but in 1944 the hotel was chosen as the site for the now famous Bretton Woods Monetary Conference, which established the gold and financial standards of the international markets in the postwar years. The U.S. government helped restore the hotel at this time, and it experienced a resurgence in popularity. But changing modes of transportation and lifestyles contributed to a slow decline in the hotel's operations by the 1960s.

New life and money were again pumped into the hotel in the late 1970s and early 1980s. Then after a series of ownership changes, which eventually resulted in the Federal Deposit Insurance Corporation taking control of the facility, a group of local business operators, including the owners of the nearby Mt. Washington Cog Railway, purchased the hotel and its adjacent property at a 1991 FDIC auction. Since then, the local ownership group has undertaken an ambitious renovation strategy which has included the modernization of guest accommodations. All the while, the hotel has retained the grace and elegance of the grand hotel era and the Mount Washington Hotel continues to thrive. There is even talk that the hotel–which is open only from May to October–may some day soon be operational on a year-round basis.

Notch House and Crawford House

In 1828, Ethan and Abel Crawford constructed a large inn just above the Gateway of the Notch, between Saco Lake and Elephant's Head (a notable rock formation on the north side of the Gateway). This hotel, called the Notch House, opened in January 1829 under the management of Thomas J. Crawford, another

OPPOSITE PAGE: *The grandest of all the magnificent White Mountain hotels, the Mount Washington, as it looked in its early years of operation.*
(PHOTO COURTESY LITTLETON AREA HISTORICAL SOCIETY)

Horse-drawn coaches line up in front of the historic Crawford House more than a century ago.
(PHOTO COURTESY LITTLETON AREA HISTORICAL SOCIETY)

of Abel's sons. It soon became a popular year-round inn and tavern and among its most distinguished guests was Henry David Thoreau, who stayed there along with his brother during his first visit to the White Mountains in 1839.

Around 1850, Thomas Crawford began work on the building of another hotel at the top of the Notch, but ran into severe financial problems and was forced to sell the Notch House and the other new unfinished building to a syndicate headed by Littleton businessman Ebenezer Eastman. The new owners completed work on the new inn, opening it for business in 1852. They also undertook some restoration work on the older Notch House, which was used primarily for overflow guests at the newer inn. Just a year after Eastman's death in 1853, the Notch House perished in a fire.

Under the able proprietorship of Col. Joseph Gibbs, the new Crawford House prospered, but like its sister inn less than a half-mile away, it too fell victim to fire on April 30, 1859. Remarkably, a replacement structure was constructed in just over two months time, with Col. Cyrus Eastman of Littleton having completed preliminary drawings of the new hotel just 48 hours after the original inn had burned to the ground. Work began on the new hotel on May 10 and by mid-July, the second Crawford House, still under Col Gibbs' management, was taking in summer tourists.

The new Crawford House was a magnificent structure, very large and stoutly built to withstand the harsh Notch winds and weather. Accommodating up to 400 guests, it was regaled as a "good hotel of the first class" in the 1887 edition of *Chisholm's White Mountain Guide-Book.* The hotel's clientele included many famous politicians, artists and scientists, including U.S. Presidents Franklin Pierce, Ulysses S. Grant, Rutherford B. Hayes, James A. Garfield, and Warren G. Harding. Remarkably, Charles A. Merrill, son of longtime Crawford House manager C.H. Merrill, held the record of returning to the grand hotel every year of his 92 years of life.

The Crawford House continued to serve the public, under several different owners, for 117 years with few physical changes to the building. For the better part of its existence it was owned by the Barron family, which purchased the hotel from the Gibbs consortium in 1872 and remained its owners until 1947. In fact it was under the guidance of Col. William Barron, its manager for more than 40 years, that the hotel reached its peak fame as one of New England's top summer resorts in the first part of this century.

Col. Barron held on to the hotel until 1947, when it was sold to a syndicate that included Brunson S. McCutcheon of Princeton, N.J., Henry Haynes of Lake Placid, N.Y., W.J. Hammond of New York City and Floridian Ricard Edgerton. The McCutcheon group owned the Crawford House for the next 20 years, then donated the entire property to Mary Hitchcock Memorial Hospital in Hanover in the early days of 1967. Just a few weeks after taking ownership of the hotel, the hospital sold it on January 23, 1967 to a pair of local businessmen, former U.S. ambassador Robert Hill and longtime hotel manager George McAvoy, both of Littleton and both officers with the newly formed People's National Bank of Littleton.

By the mid-1970s, unfortunately, the handwriting was on the wall for the great mountain resort, and in April 1976, Hill and McAvoy announced the hotel would not open for the summer season because of declining patronage and high fuel costs associated with the Arab oil embargo of 1973. In late July of 1976 the contents of the building were auctioned off–an event one North Country writer likened to a funeral–and on November 20, 1977 the vacant structure caught fire and was totally destroyed, despite the efforts of 50 area firefighters from several northern New Hampshire communities.

Today the site of the Crawford House is owned by the Appalachian Mountain Club, which purchased it in 1979 from McAvoy and the estate of the late Ambassador Hill. An additional 469 acres of forested land near the Crawford House site were turned over to the U.S. Forest Service for inclusion in the White Mountain National Forest several years earlier.

At the AMC-owned site, the Crawford House carriage house still stands, as does the nearby railroad depot, which was built in 1891 and restored to its original appearance by AMC work crews in 1984 and 1985. Inside the train depot–which is listed on the National Register of Historic Places–is a small museum and display on the history of the Crawford House. AMC also maintains a hostel and several small cabins on the hotel grounds. One of the buildings owned by AMC is the small studio built exclusively for Boston artist Frank H. Shapleigh in the latter part of the 19th century. Shapleigh's association with the Crawford House began in 1877 and continued into the middle part of the 1890s. He summered annually at the hotel and served as the Crawford House's artist-in-residence.

A Grand Way of Life

The grand hotels of the Crawford Notch region—the Crawford House, the Mount Pleasant, the Fabyan House, and the Mount Washington Hotel—provided a sumptuous lifestyle for their well-heeled clientele. Guests would arrive by trains from the big Eastern cities with servants and steamer trunks sufficient for a summer-long sojourn. Names such as Rockefeller, Woolworth, Barnum, Pullman and Astor could be found in the area's hotel registers, along with the signatures of several U.S. Presidents.

The hotels were like miniature cities in the mountains, offering every comfort and convenience for their cosmopolitan guests. The solicitous innkeepers, like captains on luxury cruise ships, left no detail unattended. The Mount Washington

Guests of the luxurious Crawford House are taught the finer points of lawn bowling.

even provided a private wire so guests could keep tabs on the stock market.

The meals at the grand hotels were gastronomic epics, prepared by some of the nation's top chefs. Low-cholesterol diets were nowhere in evidence. The day's progression of prodigious meals would culminate with a formal, multi-course dinner of several hours' duration. A favorite after-dinner pastime was rocking on the veranda and watching other guests stroll by in their evening finery.

When not lifting fork to mouth, guests enjoyed an endless round of leisurely pursuits: tennis, golf, mountain climbing, wagon rides, horseback riding and genteel sports such as badminton, bowling and croquet. Railroad excursions and, later, automobile touring to scenic points, were popular diversions. Some of the hotels sponsored baseball teams composed of top college players, and the games were attended by large and enthusiastic crowds.

Each hotel had its resident orchestra and dance instructor. Evenings brought dances, plays, concerts, lectures and card parties. Special events included grand balls and cotillion, and parades of horse-drawn coaches bedecked with elaborate decorations.

The cost for indulging in all this luxury was some $3.00 to $6.00 a day at the turn of the century, with weekly rates from $12.00 to $35.00. You can still sample this grand way of life at the area's only surviving grand hotel, the proud Mount Washington, but you'll find the rates a bit higher in the 1990s!

Willey House

Three miles below the top of the Notch, a Mr. Davis built a small one and a half story house along the Saco River in 1792 or 1793. Shortly after, Henry Hill opened the house as a waystation for travelers through the Notch. In 1825, after being unoccupied for several months, Samuel Willey moved his family and two hired hands onto the property. They reopened the house to guests, but one year later all perished in the great landslide of 1826, although the house itself was untouched by the disaster.

For the next 18 years, the Willey House was unoccupied much of the time as the lonely and desolate nature of the place discouraged people from living in or operating the house. In 1844, Portland, Maine businessman and area hotel operator Horace Fabyan purchased the property, and after renovating the old house, built a large inn adjacent to the Willey House, which became known as the Willey House Hotel.

The mountain hostel, obviously still a curiosity to visitors, remained open for several decades, but on a Saturday night in late September of 1899, a fire, believed to have been caused by a defective chimney, flattened both the old Willey home and the larger addition. In a report on the fire in its September 27, 1899 edition, the *Littleton Courier* newspaper said, "All occupants were obliged to make harried exits. Several were unable to dress and rushed from the burning building in their night clothes." Two of the inn's owners, Mr. and Mrs. Henry Leonard, were at the Willey House when the fire struck. "They were awakened by one of their employees, who had discovered the fire, and an effort was at once made to subdue the flames. This was unavailing and the structure was rapidly consumed," reported the paper.

Samuel Bemis' grand stone cottage, built between 1852 and 1862, is operated today as the Notchland Inn.

(PHOTO BY AUTHOR)

Today the Willey House site is part of Crawford Notch State Park, and a small plaque and memorial mark the site of the former structure.

Notchland Inn

Between 1856 and 1862, Dr. Samuel Bemis, a wealthy Boston dentist, built a large stone house in the style of an English country manor. Dr. Bemis, an old acquaintance of Abel Crawford and his son-in-law, Nathaniel T.P. Davis, built his mountain home near the aging Mount Crawford House, overlooking it from a small knoll west of the former Crawford residence. The granite blocks used in the construction of the manor were quarried from a site along the nearby Sawyer River, a few miles to the south.

Dr. Bemis, through foreclosure proceedings, acquired the old Crawford farm property and tavern from Davis a few month's after Crawford's death in 1851. Upon Bemis' death in 1880, the manor and extensive Bemis land holdings were willed to his friend and longtime property superintendent, George Morey.

The Morey family owned the property for nearly a century. George Morey's eldest son, Charles, inherited the home after his father's death in 1902. In 1920, Charles Morey's bride, former Boston socialite Florence Worth Prendergast, opened the old Bemis house to the public and operated it as the Notchland Inn. Florence Morey soon became known as the "Lady of the Manor" as she operated her mountain inn for more than 40 years. She would also prove to be a powerful and influential woman, eventually becoming one of the state's first women legislators.

The Notchland Inn's name was changed at some point in time to the Inn Unique, and Mrs. Morey managed it until she became too elderly for the day-to-day tasks. Following Mrs. Morey's death in 1978, many historic relics of the Notch, stored and on display in the manor, were auctioned off (in 1980) to settle substantial family debts.

After being closed to the public for several years, the building was reopened as an inn (in 1984) by new owners John and Pat Bernardin. They later renamed it the Notchland Inn, and the house and grounds underwent some restoration and improvements. The Notchland Inn's current owners are Ed Butler and Ed Schoof, who purchased the building in 1993. It remains open for business year-round, carrying on the tradition of mountain hospitality in Crawford Notch.

English Jack—Hermit of the Notch

John Alfred Vials, more commonly known as "English Jack" or the "Hermit of the White Mountains," is perhaps the most intriguing, and certainly most unusual character to ever be connected with Crawford Notch. Vials, an Englishman who came to the White Mountains to help with construction of the railroad through Crawford Notch in the mid-1870s, lived for many summers in a ramshackle hut in the woods near the Gateway to the Notch.

Known for his spellbinding tales of adventures—be it fighting to free slaves in Africa or soldiering in the Crimean and Indian border wars—English Jack was a big hit with area ho-

English Jack, the Hermit of the White Mountains, is pictured in front of his ramshackle summer home near the Gateway of the Notch in this turn-of-the-century postcard.
(POSTCARD COURTESY OF CRAWFORD NOTCH STATE PARK)

tel guests who would flock to his decrepit shanty to hear him relate one of his yarns, or perhaps sample some of the special beer he brewed out of hops and roots that grew in the woods near his dwelling.

Ever the salesman, English Jack made money out of his spartan existence by selling to visiting tourists postcards depicting himself and "The House that Jack Built." Another popular souvenir item he peddled was a booklet of his life story written in rhyme by James E. Mitchell and published first in 1891.

His engaging, if not downright unusual lifestyle, also included a diet of snakes, which he would, on occasion, gulp down in front of visitors from the nearby Crawford House. No doubt behavior such as this only further enhanced his already legendary status amongst Crawford Notch visitors.

English Jack lived to the ripe old age of 90, and spent winters in the latter part of his life living with the William McGee family of nearby Twin Mountain. He died in 1912.

NINE

Modern Hospitality Offerings

Overnight accommodations in and around the Crawford Notch area run the gamut from the grand Mount Washington Hotel in Bretton Woods to the Appalachian Mountain Club's Crawford Hostel on the grounds of the former Crawford House at the top of the Notch.

The red-roofed Mount Washington Hotel, the grand lady of the great old-time White Mountain resorts, operates on a seasonal basis from mid-May to mid-October, but its owners are seriously considering making it a year-round facility by the start of the new millennium. The landmark 200-room hotel offers a step back into the gilded age, and recent renovations to the near century-old structure have added modern conveniences without compromising its elegance and tradition. Resort facilities include 27 holes of golf, a dozen tennis courts, indoor and outdoor swimming pools, a riding stable, and the hotel's grand dining room. For reservations or other information, call 603-278-1000 or 800-258-0330 (outside N.H.).

The rejuvenated hotel is but one entity of the Bretton Woods Resort property. Other lodging establishments close by include: the restored Bretton Arms Country Inn, built in 1896, completely renovated a decade ago, and now offering 34 rooms and suites for visitors; the modern Bretton Woods Motor Inn, with 50 guest rooms, an indoor pool, and stunning views of the grand hotel across the way and the peaks of the Presidential Range; the 14-unit Above the Notch Motor Inn; and dozens of townhouse and condominium rental units scattered about the Bretton Woods area.

The Crawford Hostel just above the Gateway to the Notch caters to the hiking and outdoors crowd, offering bunkroom accommodations, fee showers, and a self-service kitchen. It is open year-round and is situated perfectly for recreationists planning to hike or ski the trails along the nearby Willey Range or the southern Presidentials. Overnight lodging information may be obtained by calling AMC at 603-466-2727.

The Notchland Inn, which has catered to overnight guests for more than 75 years, is the lone inn or hotel in the southern reaches of the Notch. The elegant 1860 granite mansion offers 11 guest rooms, all with working fireplaces and private baths. For reservations or other information, call 800-866-6131 or 603-374-6131

During the warmer months of the year, two campground facilities offer cruder accommodations for those so inclined. The state-run Dry River Campground is on the east side of Route 302, about a half-mile from the southern entrance to the state park. It has 30 primitive tent sites, but few conveniences other than running water and pit toilets. Starting with the 1997 camping season, sites at the state-run campground may be reserved in advance by calling 603-271-3268 between the hours of 9 a.m. and 4 p.m., or by writing to: New Hampshire Division of Parks. P.O. Box 1856, Concord, NH 03302.

Two miles to the south of Dry River Campground is the privately-run Crawford Notch General Store and Campground with 75 sites, including several alongside the scenic Saco River.

TEN

Geology of the Notch

Born of an inland sea, crumpled by continental collisions, worn for eons by water, frost and wind, sculpted by great sheets of ice–the White Mountains and Crawford Notch attest to the vastness and variety of the earth's geologic forces.

The geology of Crawford Notch has been painstakingly pieced together by scientists, though many uncertainties remain. It is a complex story that spans vast periods of time. The bedrock that makes up the mountains and underlies the valleys is very old; some dating back 400 million years. [By comparison, the bedrock of New York's Adirondack Mountains and Vermont's Green Mountains is more ancient still–some a billion years old–while the Rocky Mountains of the American West are much younger at a mere 70 million years.] Countless centuries of erosion, interspersed early on with periods of intense mountain-building activity, have exposed these venerable rocks and shaped the topography we see today.

About 400 million years ago (MYA), the White Mountain region was covered by a shallow inland sea. Erosion of ancient mountain ranges deposited thousands of feet of mud, silt, and sand on the ocean floor. As the sediments accumulated, they were compressed to form layered sedimentary rock–mainly shales and sandstones–known as the Littleton Formation.

About 380 MYA the area underwent a period of severe folding, known as the "Acadian Revolution." Recent theories attribute this to the slow, inexorable collision of the drifting North American and Eur-African continental plates. This titanic fusion brought intense heat (about 1,000 degrees Fahrenheit) and pressure to bear upon the soft sedimentary rocks. As the shales and sandstones were heated and squeezed, they recrystallized into the metamorphic ("changed") rocks called gneiss, schist, and quartzite.

These metamorphic rocks are as tough and resistant as any rock in New England. They make up the entire Presidential Range: gneiss in the Southern Peaks and Mount Clay, mica schist and quartzite in Mounts Washington, Jefferson, Adams and Madison. (Ironically, the highest peaks in the Granite State are not made of granite.)

A trademark of these metamorphic rocks is their conspicuous folding, giving them a rugged, contorted appearance. The gneiss of this period is well-exposed on the cliff of Elephant Head and other outcroppings at the Gateway of the Notch. Interbedded quartzite and schist are found on Mount Willey, on the west side of the Notch, and can be seen along the railroad tracks on either side of the Willey Brook trestle.

About 375 MYA, the Acadian Revolution continued with great upwellings of magma (molten rock) beneath the earth's surface. The magma cooled and crystallized at a depth of several miles. In the Crawford Notch area, this igneous ("firemade") rock is represented by a large body of Concord quartz monzonite extending north from Saco Lake and the northern slopes of Mount Willard.

A long period of erosion followed the Acadian Revolution. For 185 million years, water, frost, and wind combined to wear down a layer of rock seven miles thick. The rate of erosion was painfully slow—about two feet every 10,000 years. A gentle uplift accompanied this gradual scalping of the land, meaning that the mountains of millennia ago may have been no higher than those we see today.

The second phase in the formation of the region's bedrock began about 190 MYA with a series of volcanic eruptions, caused by the tearing apart of the North American and Eur-African continents. At one time, nearly all of New Hampshire may have been blanketed by a layer of volcanic rock. Most of this, though, was subsequently eroded away. Today, these "Moat Volcanics" remain in a narrow band along the crest of the Willey Range, on either side of Mount Tom, and especially in the Moat Mountains near North Conway, 20 miles southeast of Crawford Notch.

A great underground intrusion of magma followed the volcanic eruptions. As the molten rock cooled, a series of granitic rocks crystallized some four miles beneath the surface. The most widespread rock of this period, Conway granite, forms most of the floor and walls of Crawford Notch–including the great Webster Cliffs–and much of the terrain to the west. Conway granite is easily recognized by its coarse grains and distinctive pink color. Another rock formed at this time, Mount Osceola granite, is well-exposed on Frankenstein Cliff at the south end of the Notch.

At this point, about 185 MYA, all of the region's bedrock had been formed. Again there were millions of years of erosion, and about four more miles of rock were worn away. To the east, many geologists believe that the Presidential Range area was eroded to a low, rolling surface called a "peneplain." Mount Washington rose perhaps 1,000 feet above this plateau. A similar level area, the Frankenstein Surface, formed to the west.

Remnants of the Presidential peneplain are seen today as level "lawns" at the base of the summit cone of Mount Washington. Likewise, the Frankenstein Surface can be discerned as a relatively flat area, about 2,600 feet high, west of Frankenstein Cliff.

Two subsequent uplifts, probably less than 20 MYA, raised the region's land surface several thousand feet. This caused streams to flow much faster and erode more deeply. The basic topography we see today was shaped by this last relatively short period of erosion, dependent largely on the structure and relative hardness of the various types of bedrock.

Two million years ago, the mountains looked much the same as today. It remained for the glaciers to add the finishing touches to the White Mountain landscape and to carve the spectacular scenery of Crawford Notch.

For reasons unknown, the earth's climate cooled markedly. As snow and ice built up year after year, alpine glaciers formed in the ravines on the eastern and northern slopes of the Presidentials. These local glaciers hollowed out bowl-shaped valleys with steep headwalls.

The most famous of these "cirques" is Tuckerman Ravine near Pinkham Notch. Closer to Crawford Notch is Oakes Gulf, located on the south side of Mount Washington and visible from the viewpoint on U.S. Route 302 near the Arethusa Falls parking area at the south entrance to Crawford Notch State Park. The cirques contrast with the stream-carved, V-shaped ravines found on the western slopes of the range (those facing towards Bretton Woods).

The classic U-shaped valley of the Saco River and Crawford Notch, as seen from the summit of Mount Avalon.

(PHOTO BY AUTHOR)

Mountain glaciers did not form on the west side because much snow was blown off by prevailing westerly winds.

Eventually a great continental ice sheet flowed ponderously down from Canada. There were probably several advances and retreats during the Ice Age, but geologists can read only the last glacier's record. The final glacier was over a mile thick, and even Mount Washington's summit vanished beneath the ice. For centuries, an eerie blue-white landscape prevailed over the entire region.

Crawford Notch is a textbook example of a glaciated valley. Indeed, it has served as an illustration for many a treatise on glaciology. The striking u-shaped trough was created when the ice sheet, following the path of least resistance, ground its way through what was then a U-shaped valley. The tremendous force of the ice flow deepened the valley by as much as 500 feet and smoothed and steepened the walls.

Many other signs of glaciation are evident around the Notch. The peaks of the Southern Presidentials were rounded by the southeast-flowing glacier. These mountains and especially Mount Willard show "stoss-and-lee" topography–gentle slopes on the northwest side, where the glacier flowed uphill, and precipitous slopes on the southeast side, caused by the plucking action of the ice as it moved downhill.

Glacial scratches and striations, gouged by rocks embedded in the moving ice, may be seen on many areas of exposed bedrock. Glacial "erratics"–boulders from miles away deposited by the ice–are found nearly to the summit of Mount Washington. Erratics are especially noticeable when their composition differs from that of the ledge or outcrop where they now reside.

Much of the soil in the area (and in all of New England) is glacial till–an unsorted mixture of rocks, sand, and clay left behind when the last ice sheet melted away. Sandy deposits from glacial meltwater are common in the Bretton Woods valley north of Crawford Notch.

The last continental glacier receded some 12,000 years ago, but frost action has continued in the mountains. In the severe climate of the post-glacial era, water freezing and thawing in bedrock fractures created the jumbles of angular rocks found on the cones of the higher Presidential Range peaks. The wedging force of freeze-thaw cycles is still at work today, though on a smaller scale.

Evidence of current geologic activity is seen in the gashes of landslides on many steep, forested slopes, such as the west face of Mount Webster and the west-facing ravines of the Presidential Range peaks. Slides occur where the gradient is steep (30 or 40 degrees) and soil cover is thin. A heavy rainstorm is the catalyst which brings vegetation, soil, and rock plummeting down a mountainside. The famous 1826 slide that buried the Willey family was caused by a torrential downpour following a prolonged dry spell.

Though the mountains seem changeless today, the relentless forces of erosion continue to wear down the summits and deposit sediments in the valleys, and, ultimately, the sea. The geologic story of Crawford Notch is unimaginably old, but the tale is certainly not yet complete.

For a sweeping overview of Crawford Notch geology, take the relatively easy 1.6 mile hike to the summit of Mount Willard. Along the first half of the trail, you walk over Concord Quartz Monzonite, 375 million years old, overlain with glacial till and a layer of topsoil formed since the last ice sheet melted away. Halfway up, you leap forward 190 million years in geologic time and cross onto Conway Granite formed some 185 MYA.

From the open ledges at Mount Willard's summit, you are treated to a breathtaking view of the u-shaped Notch. Far below you see the parallel stripes of Route 302 and the railroad line, and, to your left, the course of the Saco River. The cliffs of Mount Webster form the left wall; the steep slopes of Mount Willey, scarred by landslides, are on the right. On the far left are Mount Washington and the Presidentials, made of metamorphic rock nearly 400 million years old.

(Much of the information in the preceding section is based on the booklet, *The Geology of the Crawford Notch Quadrangle* by Donald M. Henderson.)

ELEVEN

Plants and Wildlife

The Crawford Notch area is furnished with a fascinating variety of vegetation and wildlife. This diversity is largely due to the elevation differences between mountains and valleys. At this latitude, every 1,000-foot rise in altitude produces the same climatic effect as traveling about 230 miles north. In terms of average temperature, there is a drop of about three and a half degrees Fahrenheit for every 1,000 feet up. In general, higher elevations have a colder, wetter, windier climate and a shorter growing season than the lowlands. Thus as one ascends a mountainside, the plant and animal life take on a more northerly character, progressing from the temperate to the arctic. Fewer species are found in the harsher environment of high elevations.

VEGETATION:

The continental ice sheets scoured the land clean of all vegetation. As the last glacier receded slowly northward at the end of the Ice Age, a band of arctic-like tundra followed the melting edge of the ice. South of the tundra, the forests reoccupied the land, with spruce and fir in the lead and the northern hardwoods behind. These three major plant associations–northern hardwoods, spruce-fir, and tundra–dominate the vegetation of the White Mountains today, and are arrayed into "zones" on the mountainside in response to altitudinal differences in climate. (In the lower river valleys, such as the Saco valley around Bartlett and North Conway, a more southerly oak-white pine forest is found).

However, many factors besides climate have contributed to

the vegetative pattern we see in the mountains today. These factors include: type of soil and bedrock, topography and exposure, fire, windstorms (such as the destructive Hurricane of 1938), landslides, insect and disease epidemics, and, of course, man. All but the most inaccessible forests in the White Mountains have been logged at least once; thus there is little virgin forest in the area. One notable exception is the Gibbs Brook Scenic Area on the east side of the Notch, which contains a fine stand of old-growth red spruce. The old-growth forest is characterized by trees in all stages of growth and decay, in contrast to the relatively even-aged composition of second-growth forests. Some of the trees in the Gibbs Brook stand are 80 to 90 feet tall, with trunks over two feet thick. The Crawford Path hiking trail passes through this stand, providing a glimpse of what the mountain forests were like before the loggers plied their often ruthless trade. Other old-growth spruce forests are found atop Frankenstein Cliff and in the Nancy Pond Area. Both are in the lower part of the Notch and are accessible by hiking trail. The Nancy Brook stand is among the largest virgin forests in New Hampshire.

The logging era of the late 1800s and early 1900s was a colorful period in White Mountain history. Logging roads and railroads crisscrossed the region, and many present-day hiking trails follow these routes. Clearings along the trails mark the sites of former lumber camps and even entire villages. Unfortunately, some timber barons were prone to "cut out and get out," leaving denuded slopes and piles of tinder-dry slash. A series of fires devastated much of the area between Crawford Notch and Franconia Notch, and a public outcry ensued. The Society for the Protection of New Hampshire Forests and other organizations lobbied for legislation to protect the forests, and in 1911 Congress passed the Weeks Act, authorizing the purchase of National Forest lands in the East.

Today, more than 770,000 acres of the White Mountain National Forest are managed by the U.S. Forest Service for recreation, timber, water, and wildlife purposes. Most of the scars caused by logging abuses have healed, and once again the region is covered with a thick and lush–though perhaps markedly different–forest. The most remarkable regeneration has occurred in the scenic Zealand Valley, west of the Willey and Rosebrook ranges. Two fires (in 1886 and 1903) devastated this valley, leaving little but charred rock. Yet today the valley supports a fine forest of second-growth hardwoods and conifers, with many beautiful groves of white birch.

Although there are countless local variations in habitat, the altitudinal patterns in plant life are evident as one ascends from the floor of the Notch. The passenger or hiker who climbs one of the higher Presidential Range peaks will notice a progression of vegetation "zones." These are northern hardwoods, transition, spruce-fir, "krummholz", and highest of all, the open, windswept alpine tundra.

The floor of the Notch and the lower slopes of the mountains, up to about 2,000 feet, are covered with the beautiful northern hardwood forest. It is this forest which produces the North Country's stunning autumnal display of colors. Three trees predominate in the moist, rich soil: yellow birch, with shiny silver bark peeling in thin strips; sugar maple, in a taller, slimmer form than the familiar dooryard maple; and American beech, recognized by its smooth gray bark. Route 302 traverses northern hardwood forest for several miles along the floor of the Notch. The Mount Clinton Road, connecting the Cog Railway Base Road and U.S. Route 302 near the top of the Notch, passes through a cool and shady northern hardwood forest. Alongside brooks and in steep, shady ravines, conifers often predominate, even on the valley floor. These include hemlock, white pine, red spruce and balsam fir.

Between 2,000 and 3,000 feet (these boundaries are not sharp) is a transition zone from the northern hardwood forest to the coniferous forest of higher elevations. Beech and sugar maple drop out, and more and more conifers—primarily red spruce and balsam fir—enter the forest. Paper birch is common here, often occurring in pure groves. At higher elevations a reddish-barked mountain variety—the heart-leafed paper birch—is found. Paper birch is a fast-growing "pioneer species" that thrives in places where the forest has been disturbed by fire, logging, or windthrow. Birch groves often have an understory of young spruce and fir trees. The shade-tolerant conifers will eventually replace the sun-loving birches.

Two smaller trees common in the transition zone are striped maple (or moosewood) and mountain ash (with sumac-like leaves, not a true ash). A characteristic shrub of both the hardwood and transition forests is hobblebush, identified by its long tendrils of large, heart-shaped leaves. In early summer it bears showy clusters of white flowers; in late summer these ripen into dark berries.

Many woodland flowers may be found on the lower mountain slopes. Red and painted trilliums are among the most beautiful spring flowers. Clintonia, or bluebead lily, has delicate pale-yellow flowers, and bears deep blue berries in late summer. Pink lady's slippers, goldthread, starflower, purple twisted stalk, foamflower, common wood sorrel, bunchberry, Canada mayflower, and various violets are also common.

Many flowers bloom early in the hardwood forest, taking advantage of the sun before the leaf canopy closes in overhead. Flowers with a wide altitudinal range, such as bunchberry and Clintonia, may be in several different stages of bloom along the same trail. For these particular plants, spring and flowering come later at high elevations. In addition to the flowers, there is a wide variety of ferns, mosses, lichens, and fungi on the forest floor.

The upper slopes of the mountains, above 3,000 feet, are cloaked with thick forests of red spruce and balsam fir, mixed with the heart-leaved birch and mountain ash. Spruce and fir can be distinguished with a simple test: Spruce needles can be rolled between thumb and forefinger, while the flat needles of the fir cannot. The conifers are well adapted to the thin, acidic, nutrient-poor soil and cold, wet climate at higher elevations. The coniferous woods are often dark and gloomy, in marked contrast to the airy, sun-dappled deciduous woods below. In some places mosses, ferns, and carpets of wood sorrel lend rain forest lushness to the forest floor. Typical flowers of the spruce-fir forest include goldthread, bunchberry and Canada mayflower. Over the years, high winds have caused many areas of "blowdowns" among the shallow-rooted conifers. An interesting phenomenon is the "fir wave," a band of dead balsams that shows as a wavy gray stripe on the mountainside when seen from a distance. The zone of dead trees apparently moves up the slope at a rate of several feet per year. The trees are killed by wind, icing and other stresses of life at the higher elevations. Fir waves are especially prominent around the summit of Mount Tom in the Willey Range.

Above 4,000 feet in elevation, the conifers (at this altitude consisting largely of the more prolific balsam fir) diminish in size, until they have become grotesquely stunted and contorted. Treeline generally occurs between 4,800 and 5,200 feet—lower on exposed northern and western slopes, higher on protected southern and eastern slopes. Trees cannot survive above this elevation because of the intense wind and cold. At and near treeline, the trees grow in low, thick, twisted mats called "krummholz"– German for "crooked wood." The krummholz trees are mainly balsam fir and black spruce; the latter tree replaces red spruce near the treeline. There are also some gnarled birches among the krummholz.

Some of these diminutive trees may be over a hundred years old. Krummholz growth is mainly horizontal and low to the ground, where winter snow provides moisture and protection from the wind and cold. Vertical growth is quickly killed by the battering and drying effects of the wind. In the leeward shelter of a rock, the krummholz may be two or three feet high, while in an exposed area a few feet away, the trees may be only ten to twelve inches high. Although the krummholz is very dense–early explorers reportedly walked atop it to reach the higher summits–it is also fragile, and campsites hacked out of the trees cause an ever-widening circle of winterkill.

Above treeline is the alpine zone, nearly eight square miles of the Arctic-like tundra of which is found atop the Presidential Range. (Smaller alpine areas are found on the Franconia Range and several individual White Mountain peaks). This is a unique climatic area left in the wake of the retreating continental glacier, and it has fascinated scientists for many years. A number of geographic features along the Presidentials and near Mount Washington bear the names of early naturalists who came to study the alpine zone. Tuckerman Ravine, Huntington Ravine, Oakes Gulf, Boott Spur, and Bigelow Lawn are examples of these namesake features.

The plant life of the alpine zone is similar to that found above the continental treeline in northern Canada. These plants provide a remarkable lesson on the art of survival in a harsh environment. The growing season is short, the soil sparse and stony, the wind and cold relentless; yet one will find grasses, sedges, mosses, lichens, dwarf willows and birches, scattered patches of krummholz, and numerous colorful wildflowers (many of them from the heath family). Most of these plants hug close to the ground, where temperatures are warmer, and use snow cover and the leeward shelter of rocks for protection from the deadly drying effects of the wind. Some species have thick, waxy leaves to retard water loss. Distinct plant communities have evolved in adaptation to differing "micro-climates" above treeline. On open and windswept slopes, dense clumps of white-flowered diapensia predominate, along with Lapland rosebay and alpine azalea. In more sheltered spots, where snow accumulates deeply and melts late in the spring, the "snowbank community" is found, where some flowers from the forests below venture into these somewhat milder conditions. On the higher slopes, sedge meadows are common, with Bigelow sedge as the main component. (L.C. Bliss describes these and other alpine plant communities in his booklet, *Alpine Zone of the Presidential Range*). Hardiest of all are the crusty lichens which dot the frost-riven boulders of New Hampshire's highest peaks with greens, blacks, and yellows.

Through June and into early July, the blooms of the alpine wildflowers brighten the flat "lawns" below the summits of the higher Presidential Range peaks. Three of these flowers—dwarf cinquefoil (very rare), alpine avens, and alpine bluet—are "endemics," occurring only in the White Mountains, and, in the latter two cases, in small areas in eastern Canada. The best place to view the alpine flowers is in the Alpine Garden, located at about 5,300-feet elevation on the eastern flank of Mount Washington. Ironically, the greatest menace these hardy plants face is the Vibram-soled boots of walkers who come to admire them. In the severe conditions above treeline, plant growth and regeneration are exceedingly slow. Hikers in the alpine zone should stay on the trails to preserve this fragile environment for others to enjoy.

From the Crawford Notch area, the easiest trail accesses to the alpine zone are the Crawford Path to Mounts Pierce and Eisenhower, and the Edmands Path to Mount Eisenhower.

WILDLIFE:

The White Mountains are host to a rich diversity of wildlife, for the region is a "border ground" where the ranges of northern and southern species overlap. Perhaps 50 species of mammals occur in the region, and over 140 species of birds are known to nest in the White Mountains. The Crawford Notch area provides a wide variety of wildlife habitats—lawns, fields, brushy areas, stream banks, boggy areas, swamps, beaver ponds and meadows, hardwood and coniferous forests, cliffs, and mountaintops. Thus within a five or six-mile radius of the Willey House site, one may find most of the mammals and birds that inhabit the region.

Mammals:

A number of familiar mammals are found in the Crawford Notch area. Raccoons prowl about the riverbanks and park grounds, woodchucks are common in the fields, and snowshoe hares (brown in summer, white in winter) may be seen along the edges of the forest. Chipmunks seem to be everywhere in the hardwoods. The red squirrel, a mischievous sort, favors the deep shade of the coniferous forest, and intruders into its domain are often greeted with a long, contemptuous chatter. The nocturnal Northern flying squirrel is also found in the area.

Bats commonly feed at night around the lights of park buildings. At least six species are found in the White Mountains. There are also a number of mice, voles, moles, and shrews in the region, though most are nocturnal and infrequently seen. These smallest mammals are the only ones that regularly make their home above the treeline; some other mammals do make occasional forays from the forest below.

The work of beavers is evident along several trails in the area, especially the Sam Willey Trail. Around wet areas, looks for dams, lodges (dome-shaped piles of sticks and mud), and gnawed tree trunks. Although scarce at the turn of the century, beavers have made a remarkable comeback and are now quite common. Beaver ponds and meadows provide excellent habitat for many other forms of wildlife.

Coyotes or "coydogs" (a reputed cross between the coyote and domestic dog) have moved into the area in recent years. Night travelers along Route 302 may also spot a red fox in the glare of their headlights. Bobcats undoubtedly inhabit the woods of the valley, but are rarely sighted. Several members of the weasel family are found as well, including mink, otter, striped skunk, fisher, and short-tailed weasel. The fisher is noted for its adeptness at preying on well-armored porcupines. The short-tailed weasel, or ermine, turns snow-white in winter. Deer are also present at lower elevations in the area, although the deep snows and long winters keep their numbers relatively low.

The moose, most majestic of all the creatures of the northern

A cow moose ambles alongside Route 302 between the Gateway to the Notch and Bretton Woods resort area. Visitors will find this stretch of highway to be the best in the area for spotting moose.
(PHOTO BY AUTHOR)

forests, has made a remarkable recovery in the past quarter century. Hunted nearly to extinction in the 1800s, they were still rare in New Hampshire as late as 1950. However, moose are now abundant in the White Mountains and visitors to the Crawford Notch area have a good chance of spotting one of the great beasts. One of the best places for moose watching is an area of muddy wallows alongside Route 302 just north of the fields of the old Crawford House golf course at the top of the Notch. The best times for viewing moose are dawn and dusk. (Note: Always keep an eye peeled for moose while driving at night. They may appear on the roadway at any time and are difficult to spot because of their dark coloration.)

A large bull moose can tip the scales at over 1,000 pounds, and seeing one resplendent with a full rack of antlers is a true northwoods treat. If no moose are in sight, you may very well find evidence of their passing, especially along hiking trails: large, cloven tracks, much bigger than deer tracks; shoulder-high tooth scrapings on the bark of small hardwood trees; and mounds of big brown pellets. Some North Country entrepreneurs now sell lacquered moose droppings as novelty jewelry and ornaments!

Another large mammal that frequents the Notch is the black bear. The bear is a retiring animal and usually shies away from any contact with man. Bruins are seen on occasion though, lumbering across a darkened highway or raiding an untended dumpster near the state park headquarters at the Willey House site. You're more likely to see bear claw marks on beech trees on the floor of the Notch. Bears are excellent tree climbers and beechnuts are one of their favorite treats.

Bears are opportunistic foragers and are quite fond of campers' food, if they can get at it. Car campers are advised to secure all food in the trunk at night, and backpackers should hang all food in a "bear bag" from a projecting tree limb, at least 10 feet high and four feet from the trunk. In the early 1990s a large area bruin nicknamed "Brutus" by U.S. Forest Service rangers learned to associate backpackers with easy pickings. More than once, hikers cowered on the roof of Ethan Pond Shelter while Brutus enjoyed a leisurely meal inside the log lean-to. There have been no "Brutus" reports since 1994, but by keeping food out of reach, campers can help keep the area's bears wild and wary of humans.

Several other legendary predators were extirpated from the White Mountains many years ago: the gray wolf, the lynx (or Canada Lynx), and the mountain lion (or cougar). Ethan Allen Crawford wrote of his legendary run-ins with wolves and lynx in *History of the White Mountains,* published shortly after his death. In recent years there have been scattered but persistent reports of cougar sightings in northern New Hampshire, and a confirmed sighting in northern Vermont in 1995, though it remains uncertain whether one or more of the great cats now roams the forests of the White Mountains. Occasional reports of wolves have also surfaced (including one in nearby Jefferson), but there have been no confirmed sightings.

Birds:

The abundant bird life of the Crawford Notch area lends color and song to summer in the mountains. As many as 100 species nest in the region, while a number of others pass through during spring and fall migrations, or visit as winter wanderers.

Many birds may be seen in open roadside areas, while others must be sought deep in the woods or high in the mountains. A birding highlight of the area is the presence of a number of "northern specialties"–birds which are known only as spring and fall migrants or rare winter visitors in most of the Northeast, but which nest in these more northern climes.

Among the most conspicuous birds are the graceful swallows, which return year after year to nest under the eaves of buildings in the Notch, and also at the grand Mount Washington Hotel, a few miles north at Bretton Woods. On a summer day the air above Saco Lake at the top of the Notch is filled with their swooping, drafting forms. The Barn Swallow is distinguished by its dark blue back and deeply forked tail. The Cliff Swallow, another blue-backed species, has a buffy forehead, rusty rump, and only slightly notched tail. Cliff Swallows build interesting gourd-shaped mud nests that are plastered into nooks and crannies of buildings at the Crawford House site. Each nest is made of about a thousand mud pellets. The Green-backed Tree Swallow prefers to nest in woodpecker holes or other cavities. Occasionally a Bank Swallow (told by its brown back and breast band) may be seen. A colony of these birds sometimes nests in the gravel pit north of the top of the Notch. Squadrons of twittering Chimney Swifts (often described as "flying cigars") tirelessly patrol the sky. At dusk, the swifts funnel into chimneys (like that of the hotel) to roost for the night. Together the swallows and the swifts consume vast quantities of flying insects.

The Willey House and Crawford House grounds are home to such familiar dooryard birds as the Robin, Gray Catbird, Song Sparrow, and Common Grackle. The Starling, introduced from Europe into New York City's Central Park in 1890, nests in crevices in buildings in the Notch. Interestingly, the House Sparrow, another urban immigrant from Europe, is not found in the Notch. The tiny Ruby-throated Hummingbird, the brilliant American Goldfinch, and the drab Chipping Sparrow are also common, along with the sleek, elegant Cedar Waxwing, which is often seen around the beaver ponds of the Notch floor.

Many birds of the open are found in fields that were once the Crawford House golf course and in adjacent thickets. The American Kestrel (or Sparrow Hawk), a small falcon, uses the field as a hunting ground. It can often be seen hovering over a field, searching for rodents and large insects. The secretive Vesper Sparrow and Savannah Sparrow sometimes may be seen or heard here, and Bobolinks—a species of special concern—were reported in the 1980s. The pugnacious Eastern Kingbird, black above and white below, gives chase to trespassing crows and hawks. Red-winged Blackbirds flash their red epaulets atop bushes in swampy thickets near the Gateway. Around the ponds of the Notch, and along the Saco River, one may find water-loving birds such as the noisy Belted Kingfisher and the Spotted Sandpiper, which bobs up and down in comical fashion.

The American Woodcock and occasionally the Common Snipe may be found in the moister meadows, and spring dusks are enlivened by the remarkable courtship flights of these birds. At dusk you may also hear the distinctive hoot of the Barred Owl: "Who cooks for you? Who cooks for you-all?" The courtship of a woodland game bird, the Ruffed Grouse, is marked by the "drumming" of the male. The drumming sounds like a deep heartbeat, increasing in speed towards the end, and is produced by air passing through the feathers as the bird beats its wings. This courtship tactic is evidently successful, for large families of grouse are often encountered in the woods during the summer months.

In June and July, the woods are filled with bird song. Perhaps the most typical song of the mountains is the clear, plaintive whistle of the White-throated Sparrow. A loud and rollicking song of tinkles and trills is the Winter Wren, a diminutive bird which skulks in the tangles of the coniferous woods. A rich, rolling warble coming from the treetops is that of the Purple Finch, New Hampshire's state bird. On even the hottest summer days, the Red-eyed Vireo is a persistent singer amidst the canopy of the deciduous woods. Its endless song sounds like a robin's broken up into short, quick phrases. The Solitary Vireo sings a similar song with slower, sweeter phrases.

Dusk brings forth from the forest the haunting melodies of the thrushes. Five thrushes—all with brownish backs and spotted breasts—show an interesting altitudinal distribution in the White Mountains. The Veery and Wood Thrush have a more southerly range, and occur only at lower altitudes (below 2,000 feet). The Hermit Thrush, perhaps our most noted songster, is found up to about 3,000 feet. The abundant Swainson's Thrush prefers middle altitudes, from 2,000 to 4,000 feet, while the Bicknell's Thrush is restricted to higher elevations, between 3,000 feet and treeline. There is considerable overlap in these altitudinal ranges, and

A rascally Gray Jay grabs a snack out of the hands of Steve Smith as he stands atop the snow-covered summit of Mount Jackson.
(PHOTO BY AUTHOR)

sometimes the first four thrushes listed above may all be heard singing at the top of the Notch.

The area's richest birding treasure is its abundance of warblers–small, active, brightly colored gems from the tropics. About 20 species of warblers may nest in the Crawford Notch area and some of these are at or near the southern limits of their breeding ranges. Nashville, Yellow, and Chestnut-sided Warblers favor brushy areas. Around beaver ponds and other wet areas one will find many Common Yellowthroats and an occasional Northern Waterthrush. Among the hardwoods are found the American Redstart, Ovenbird (which sings a loud, ringing "tea-cher, tea-cher, TEA-CHER, TEA-CHER"), and the Black-and-White and Black-throated Blue Warblers. Mixed and/or coniferous woods are home to the Yellow-rumped, Magnolia, Parula, Black-throated Green, Canada, Blackburnian, and Blackpoll Warblers. With luck, one may encounter one of the rarer northern warblers–Tennessee, Mourning, Wilson's, Bay-breasted, and Cape May. The boggy spruce and fir forest between the top of the Notch and Bretton Woods is a good area for northern warblers.

Other "northern specialties" found around Crawford Notch

include the Olive-sided and Yellow-bellied Flycatchers, Ruby-crowned Kinglet, Philadelphia Vireo, Rusty Blackbird, and the rare Lincoln's Sparrow. In the spruce-fir forests high on the mountainsides, birds characteristic of the Canadian north woods occur: the rascally Gray Jay (formerly Canada Jay), also known as "whiskey jack" and "camp robber," which will often take food from a hiker's hand; the ridiculously tame Spruce Grouse, or "fool hen"; the Boreal Chickadee (a brown-capped relative of the familiar Black-capped Chickadee); and the rare Black-backed or possibly the Three-toed woodpecker. The Nancy Pond and Ethan Pond areas are especially good for many of these northern species.

At the higher elevations, the Yellow-rumped and Blackpoll Warblers are abundant, with the Blackpoll's sibilant song seeming to come from every bend in the trail. The Bicknell's Thrush inhabits the stunted tree growth below treeline. Only three birds are known to nest above treeline–the White-throated Sparrow, the American Pipit, and the Northern Junco. All three are also common in the forest below.

The Common Raven, a haunter of remote cliffs and ledges, may be sighted flying over the Notch. It looks like a large Crow with a wedge-shaped tail, and utters a variety of low, hoarse croaks. Ravens often soar like hawks, and they are commonly seen gamboling in the wind around the summits. A Broad-winged or Red-tailed Hawk is also seen sometimes soaring high in the sky. A new summer resident in the region is the Turkey Vulture, which has been extending its range northward. It soars on V-shaped wings, looking a bit tipsy in its flight. In recent years, the endangered Peregrine Falcon has also been reintroduced into the White Mountains and this magnificent hawk has nested for several years on various cliffs in Crawford Notch, including those on Mount Willard and at the Frankenstein Cliffs. Please heed all signs posting areas off limits during the peregrine nesting season.

TWELVE

White Mountain Weather

"If you don't like the weather, wait a minute!"

This old New England adage is especially relevant to Crawford Notch and the entire White Mountain region, where storm tracks and air masses meet to create some of the most changeable weather anywhere. Many a cold, drizzly, dismal morning will break into a brilliant mountain day, while on a hot afternoon, a thunderstorm may develop with appalling quickness.

The seasons are distinct, each with its own special allure. Summers in the mountains are pleasant, with high temperatures averaging 75 degrees in the valleys and 15-20 degrees cooler atop the higher summits. Nights are generally cool, even during the most unbearable heat waves. Thunderstorms, raging in the mountains and bellowing through the Notch, bring much of the summer's precipitation. Fall brings the colorful foliage season, clear and crisp days, and early snowfall on the mountains. The peak of the fall color spectacle generally arrives about the last week of September at the top of Crawford Notch and a week later in the lower reaches. Winter comes early in the Whites, bringing heavy snows (over 150 inches a year at nearby Bretton Woods) and frequent sub-zero temperatures. Winter, however, is also a time of unparalleled beauty. Spring, or at least the first two-thirds of it, tends to be blustery, muddy, and unpredictable, and snow may linger high in the mountains well into summer.

While summer in the mountains is short and lush with life, winter is long and harsh, and all life in the Notch must adapt to its changing conditions of snow, rain, ice, blasting winds, and tree-snapping cold spells.

Fall is a time of preparation for the rigors of the coming winter. Conifer needles and stems are covered with a thick, waxy coating to prevent water loss. Long ago deciduous trees found it advantageous to drop their leaves and remain dormant through the cold months. The spectacular fall colors of the New England hardwood forest are offshoots of this winter adaptation. In response to the shorter and cooler days of autumn, a barrier is formed at the base of each leaf stalk. Green chlorophyll is not replenished, and the bright underlying pigments of the leaves are revealed. The maples produce the most vivid colors, ranging from scarlet through orange to golden yellow. The foliage display is brightest when there are sunny days and cool, but not frosty nights. The best time to view the Notch foliage is late September and early October. The yellows of the birches and aspens persist through much of October, but by the end of the month the hardwoods stand gray and naked.

Meanwhile the birds and animals of the mountains have been making their own preparations for winter. The vast majority of insect-eating birds move south to warmer climes, and the September woods are flooded with small migrating birds in drab fall plumage. Southbound hawks may be seen soaring on thermal updrafts along the mountain ridges of the Notch. Some mammals prepare for true and semi-hibernation. Bears gorge themselves on nuts and berries to build up fat reserves. Squirrels, chipmunks, and beavers store their caches of winter food. Snowshoe hares and ermine obtain their camouflaging winter coats.

Lasting snows usually come by mid or late December. The insulation provided by snow cover is a blessing for smaller plants on the forest floor. Now only the active winter inhabitants will be encountered. The food-seeking wanderings of mammals are marked by tracks and tunnels in the snow. The large, furry feet of the snowshoe hare enable it to move about in deep snow, and its tracks are frequently seen by cross-country skiers. Deer, however, are hindered when snow depth is much over 18 inches. They retreat to "yards" among coniferous trees, where snow is less deep, and browse on nearby deciduous growth. Moose, with their longer legs, fare better in deep snow than deer. Some insect-eating birds remain through winter, and small bands of chickadees, nuthatches, and woodpeckers bring cheer to the winter woods as they forage among the trees for hibernating insects and larvae. Northern seed-eating wanderers, such as the Pine and Evening Grosbeaks, Common Redpoll, Red and White-winged Crossbills, Pine Siskin, and Tree Sparrow, may be seen searching for seeds and dried fruits. Barred and Great Horned Owls are vocal on mid- and late winter nights.

Winters storms in the mountains may be incredibly fierce, but the season is often a time of hushed beauty. Snow-clad spruces and firs lend a northwoods quality to the landscape, while the bare hardwoods reveal views and contours unguessed at in summer. At night, countless stars glitter, cold and bright in the clear air. The lucky observer may see a display of Northern Lights send eerie shimmers of light across the sky. At such times of cold and primitive beauty, the works of man seem far removed from these timeless mountains.

THIRTEEN

Hiking Guide to Crawford Notch Trails

For nearly 200 years, the area around Crawford Notch has been a gathering spot for persons looking to explore the local mountains on foot. Situated as it is at the south end of the popular Presidential Range, the Crawford Notch area is a year-round draw for hikers and climbers. Offering walks for hikers of all ability levels and ages, the Notch is one of northern New Hampshire's premier hiking regions.

The following is a listing of hiking trails in and around Crawford Notch. For additional information on these trails, and others throughout the White Mountains, consult the *AMC White Mountain Guide* published by the Appalachian Mountain Club.

Crawford Path:

Known as the oldest continuously used and maintained hiking trail in the United States, the Crawford Path was constructed in 1819 by local innkeeper Abel Crawford and his legendary son, Ethan Allen Crawford.

The trail starts at the top of Crawford's, about a quarter-mile west of the Gateway. Trailhead parking is available at the nearby AMC Crawford Notch Hostel, at a smaller lot in front of the former Crawford House site, and at a major parking lot off Mount Clinton Road, one tenth of a mile from Route 302. The trail may be accessed from either Route 302, or via a short connecting trail (Crawford Connector) off Mount Clinton Road, which meets up with the main trail in 0.3 mile.

The well-worn Crawford Path climbs steadily through the

woods along Gibbs Brook, passes scenic Gibbs Falls to the left, and then continues up the western slopes of Mount Pierce (or Clinton as it was originally known). Much of the walk here is through one of the last old-growth forest stands in the White Mountains. [The Gibbs Brook Scenic Area, designated as such on October 6, 1961, is a 900-acre stand of virgin timber, consisting mostly of red spruce and balsam fir, but also some yellow birch and paper birch. The Gibbs Brook Scenic Area is a part of the larger Gibbs Brook Candidate Research Natural Area, which encompasses some 1,650 acres spreading out over the watersheds of Gibbs Brook, Silver and Flume Cascades, and Elephant Head Brook. The U.S. Forest Service purchased most of this land on March 20, 1920 from the Barron Hotel Company (owners of the nearby Crawford House). The price they paid–about $15 an acre– was considered a princely sum at that time.]

At 1.75 miles, the Mizpah Cutoff Trail enters right from AMC's Mizpah Spring Hut. The main trail continues straight ahead, slabbing the north side of Mount Pierce on easy to moderate grades until emerging above treeline at 2.75 miles, just a few hundred yards down from Mount Pierce's 4,310-foot summit.

From its junction with the Webster Cliff Trail all the way to Mount Washington, the Crawford Path remains mostly above treeline. In its next 5.5 miles, it passes over or near the summits of Mounts Franklin, Eisenhower and Monroe, while also swinging past the two Lakes of the Clouds and the Appalachian Mountain Club's namesake hut situated nearby the two high mountain tarns. The final 1.4 miles rises moderately up Mount Washington's rocky cone, reaching the mountain's often busy summit in 8.2 miles.

Important trail junctions along the route include: the Mount Eisenhower Loop, reached at 4.1 miles; the Edmands Path to Mount Clinton Road, reached at 4.6 miles; the Mount Eisenhower Trail from Dry River, reached at 4.8 miles; the Mount Monroe Loop, reached at 6.1 miles; Ammonoosuc Ravine Trail and Lakes of the Clouds Hut, reached at 6.8 miles; the Westside Trail to the northern peaks of the Presidential Range, and the Davis Path from Boott Spur and Montalban Ridge, reached at 7.7 miles.

As much of the Crawford Path is situated above treeline, and thus exposed to the elements, caution is urged of all hikers as severe storms have been known to strike quickly in the mountains at any time of the year. Always dress appropriately for above treeline travel.

AMC's Mizpah Spring Hut

Mizpah Spring Hut is one of the Appalachian Mountain Club's eight backcountry huts scattered across the White Mountains along the 2,160-mile Appalachian Trail. The hut, constructed in 1964 and opened to overnight guests in 1965, is the newest of the AMC facilities. It was built at the site of the former Mizpah Spring Shelter and is conveniently sited about halfway between AMC's Zealand Falls and Lakes of the Clouds huts.

Situated at an elevation of 3,800 feet, Mizpah Spring Hut allows for easy access to the higher summits of the Presidential Range. It lies less than a mile from the exposed summit of 4,310-foot Mount Pierce and just 1.7 miles from 4,052-foot Mount Jackson. It is also 6.2 miles from the top of Mount Washington.

The Appalachian Mountain Club's new Mizpah Spring Hut is dedicated at a 1965 ceremony.

(AUTHOR'S COLLECTION)

AMC's string of backcountry huts through the mountains dates back more than 100 years, when the club established its first overnight facility in the col, or low spot, between Mounts Madison and Adams, two peaks in the northern Presidential Range. Since the building of Madison Spring Hut in 1888, AMC has expanded its network of huts to include Lakes of Clouds Hut (at the southwest base of the cone of Mount Washington), Greenleaf Hut, Carter Notch Hut, Zealand Falls Hut, Galehead Hut, Lonesome Lake Hut in Franconia Notch State Park, and Mizpah Spring Hut. AMC also operates the Pinkham Notch Camp on Route 16 and the Crawford Hostel on Route 302 at the top of Crawford Notch.

Mizpah Spring Hut, like many of its sister huts, is open from mid-May to mid-October, and accommodates 60 guests. Nearby tent sites are also available for backpackers.

Crawford Connector:

This short connecting trail, just 0.2 mile in length, runs from the new Crawford Path parking lot off Mount Clinton Road to the main trail. It intersects the Crawford Path about 0.1 mile from its start after crossing Gibbs Brook on a wooden bridge.

The trail leaves the parking lot at its northeast corner near an information kiosk. It enters the woods briefly, then crosses Mount Clinton Road and reenters the woods. After a moderate climb, the trail levels out, crosses a seasonal stream bed on a small wooden bridge, then approaches a larger bridge over Gibbs Brook, at which point the Crawford Path is met. Just before the latter bridge is crossed, the Crawford Cliff Spur leaves left on the north side of Gibbs Brook. Much of the wooded Crawford Connector trail runs through the old Crawford House mule pasture, where burros used to take guests up Mount Willard were kept.

Crawford Cliff Spur:

This rough, 0.4 mile trail leads to a splendid west-facing outlook on the lower slopes of Mount Pierce. The trail leaves from the Crawford Connector at the point where the bridge crosses Gibbs Brook. Following along the north side of the stream, the trail runs on easy grades for 0.1 mile until reaching a short side path to The Pool (signed), a flume and pool along Gibbs Brook. From here the trail turns left and begins a steep climb over rough terrain to a fine outlook towards Crawford's, the peaks of the Willey Range, and the southernmost peaks of the nearby Rosebrook Range. The ledgy outlook now bearing the famous Crawford name has also been identified on older area maps and postcards as Eagle Cliff or the Eagle's Nest, according to Dave Govatski, a U.S. Forest Service worker and White Mountain historian.

The Historic Crawford Path

Perhaps the most famous of all trails in the White Mountains, the Crawford Path was built by Ethan Allen Crawford and his father, Abel, when it became apparent that visitors to the region were increasingly interested in trekking to the top of nearby Mount Washington.

"In the month of May four gentlemen came on horseback to visit the mountains," recalled the younger Crawford in his wife's classic 1845 book, *The History of the White Mountains.* "I gave them the best information I could. They set off together, and made the best they could of their excursion through the forests, but suffered considerable inconvenience by the thickness of the trees and brush, which would every now and then take hold of their clothes, and stop them; they returned well satisfied, notwithstanding the unfriendly brush.

"As this was the third party which had visited the mountains since I came here to live, we thought it best to cut a path through the woods; accordingly my father and I made a foot path from the Notch out through the woods, and it was advertised in the newspapers, and we soon began to have visitors."

The Crawford Path of those early days was nothing akin to today's well-maintained hiking path. It was "but a slight improvement over the old bushwhack routes" wrote Laura and Guy Waterman in their monumental history of hiking in the Northeast, *Forest and Crag.*

Just two years after establishing that first path to Mount Washington from the west, the Crawfords established a second route up the mountain, this one being fairly close to the route of the present day Cog Railway. Historians say Ethan

An old U.S. Forest Service trail sign that once led hikers onto the historic Crawford Path stands on display during the June 1994 ceremony officially dedicating the 175-year-old footpath as a National Recreation Trail. (PHOTO BY AUTHOR)

Allen Crawford preferred this new route to the older one, and used it almost exclusively when hired to guide visitors up the mountain.

In 1840, at the coaxing of one of the Crawfords' hired hands, Joseph Hall, the older trail was converted to a bridle path over which Abel Crawford, by then 74, made the first horseback ride to the summit of Mount Washington. In later years the trail fell into some disuse and was reportedly quite obscure in areas. After the establishment of the Appalachian Mountain Club in 1876, interest in hiking the peaks of the White Mountains increased, and soon the Crawford Path became a popular route once again for trampers headed onto the Presidentials.

On June 25, 1994, in the 175th anniversary year of its construction, the Crawford Path—or at least that segment running from Route 302 to the Webster Cliff Trail—was officially dedicated as a National Recreational Trail under the provisions of the 1968 National Trails System Act. The remainder of the trail up to Mount Washington is a link in the Appalachian Trail.

Saco Lake Trail:

One of the Crawford Notch region's lesser known, lesser used paths, this mixed trail- and-road loop hike circles the picturesque six-acre pond at the top of the Notch, just north of the narrow Gateway. The trail walk is just 0.3 mile in length, while the road walk alongside the pond's western shore is 0.2 mile.

Feature attractions include the darkly wooded crags and ledges known as Idlewild, the ample views westward toward the peaks of the Willey and Rosebrook Ranges, and a small canine graveyard dating back to the early years of this century.

The blue-blazed trail begins at the south end of the lake near a small parking area. It crosses the lake's outlet on a bridge, then enters the woods as it begins to circle the pond. Passing over several log bridges–guaranteed to delight young hikers–the trail soon reaches Idlewild, a two-tiered ledge from which are obtained excellent views of Saco Lake, the nearby mountains, and the former Crawford House site. Idlewild is accessed by a short, steep stone-step path which is no doubt easier to ascend than the wooden ladders once used by hotel guests to get to the top of the ledge. Iron railings stretch across the ledge to prevent visitors from falling forward.

From Idlewild the trail continues its circuit of the lake, passing over more log bridges, passing by more viewpoints, and passing near the dog graveyard, reached in 50 feet by a path to the right. The woods path ends a short distance from Saco Lake's northwest corner where there is a fine view across the water towards Mount Webster. Continue left from here along the highway for the short walk back to your vehicle.

Webster-Jackson Trail:

This rugged trail connects two of the area's higher peaks and in conjunction with the Webster Cliff Trail, provides for a nice 6.5 mile loop hike. The trail starts on the east side of Route 302 just beyond the Gateway at the top of the Notch. Parking is provided across the highway next to the railroad tracks.

The trail climbs by alternating steep and level pitches for about 1.4 miles, at which point it divides. Just 0.1 mile from the trail's start, look for the Elephant Head Spur branching off to the right, and in another half-mile look for a short side path on the right which leads in 60 yards to Bugle Cliff, a ledge towering high above Crawford Notch.

The view from atop the Elephant Head looking north toward Saco Lake, the Crawford Depot train station, and the former Crawford House site.
(PHOTO BY AUTHOR)

niles, where the trail splits, the left fork of the Webster-
ul continues 1.2 miles to Mount Jackson's partially bare
summit. The last 0.1 mile to the top is steep and rough
and can be difficult in wet and/or icy weather. The right fork
quickly drops down to Silver Cascade Brook, crosses over it, then
climbs steeply and roughly one mile to its junction with the
Webster Cliff Trail, about 0.1 mile north of Mount Webster's true
summit. Both summits, 1.4 miles apart, provide excellent viewpoints in most every direction and the two are connected by the
Webster Cliff Trail.

Elephant Head Spur:

This short, easy spur path off the Webster-Jackson Trail takes
hikers to the top of the landmark Elephant Head rock profile,
which forms the east side of the Gateway to the Notch. A pan-
oramic view of the Notch, the surrounding mountains, the old
railroad depot, and the former Crawford House site are obtained
by those perched atop the Elephant's ledgy head.

Begin your hike on the Webster-Jackson Trail, but proceed
for just 0.1 mile, where a sign will direct you right onto the spur
path to Elephant Head. The grade along this blue-blazed trail is
easy, but the footway is very damp and muddy in sections. After
a more moderate climb to the top of the ledge that forms the
Elephant Head, drop down 40 yards to an extensive open ledge
with a 180 degree view.

Mount Willard Trail:

Perhaps the most popular hiking trail in the Crawford Notch
region, this well traveled 1.6 mile path provides an easy ascent
route to the summit ledges of 2,804-foot Mount Willard. Beginning at the Crawford Depot off Route 302 at the top of the Notch,
the trail crosses over a set of railroad tracks, makes a sharp left
turn (signed) in about 100 yards, passes over several small streams,
and then begins a moderate climb for 0.6 mile before reaching
the graded remains of the former carriage road to the summit.
Midway through this initial part of the ascent, a trail sign directs
hikers to the right for a view overlooking Centennial Pool.

The final 0.9 mile of the trail follow (on easy grades) the old
carriage road, but the treadway has become increasingly rough
in recent years due to extensive washouts which have gouged a
deep rut in the middle of the path. The trail swings sharp left at

The famed view from the summit ledges of Mount Willard provides the best panorama of the Crawford Notch area.

(AUTHOR'S COLLECTION)

0.9 mile (near a muddy, wet area), then gradually veers right (south) for the final quarter-mile approach to the summit ledges. Just a couple hundred yards from the summit, the side trail to Hitchcock Flume (see below) leaves on the left.

From Willard's open summit, visitors are treated to a sweeping, unsurpassed view of the Notch. Mount Webster, seen to the left, and Mount Willey and Mount Field, sloping steeply upwards from the Notch floor to the right, rise high above Mount Willard on each side, while busy Route 302 and the rejuvenated railroad line snake their way along the lower depths of the Notch.

Moses Sweetser, describing the summit view in the 1881 edition of the popular guidebook *The White Mountains: A Handbook for Travelers*, wrote, "It has a singular beauty and quaint individuality which no other view possesses."

"To know the Notch truly," added writer Rev. Thomas Starr King, "one must go to the top of Mount Willard and look down into [the Notch]."

The sweeping summit view from Willard also includes the cone-like summit of Mount Chocorua, seen far to the south rising up sharply behind the ridge of Mount Tremont in Bartlett. Mounts Nancy and Bemis, in the southern end of the Notch, are seen to the left of Mount Willey's south shoulder.

From the easternmost ledges at the summit, the Presidential Range peaks of Mounts Jackson, Pierce, Eisenhower and Monroe can be viewed, along with the very top of Mount Washington.

Hitchcock Flume Spur:

This 0.2 mile long path diverges left off the Mount Willard Trail about 0.1 mile from its terminus at the summit. The rough and steep spur path drops down to the head of Hitchcock Flume, a 375-foot long, 30 to 60 foot high rock canyon on Mount Willard's east flank. To avoid unnecessary problems or accidents, hikers should proceed with caution when approaching the top of the flume.

Avalon Trail:

This trail to the 3,430-foot peak of Mount Avalon–an eastern spur of Mount Field with excellent summit views–runs 2.8 miles from the top of the Notch near the Crawford Depot train station up to the Willey Range, where it terminates 100 yards north of the wooded summit of Mount Field. While lower portions of this trail follow easy to moderate grades, the last mile and a half is steep and rough.

For the first couple hundred yards, the trail coincides with the Mount Willard Trail. At an informational signpost 100 yards from the railroad tracks, the trail continues straight ahead and in another tenth of a mile crosses over Crawford Brook.

After a short climb, the Cascade Loop trail (see description below) to Beecher and Pearl Cascades diverges left off the main trail. After passing by the upper end of the loop in another tenth of a mile, the Avalon Trail continues at an easy to moderate grade, staying to the right (north) of Crawford Brook for the first 0.8 mile. The grade steepens some after the brook is crossed for a second time. At 1.3 miles, the trail bears left at its junction with the A-Z Trail (for Zealand Falls) and soon begins a steep, rocky stretch leading in 0.5 mile to a col just below and to the west of Mount Avalon's sharp, rocky summit. The summit is reached by a short, steep side trail (left), which in 100 yards leads to the peak's open summit, where excellent views are obtained of Mount Webster and the floor of Crawford Notch, the peaks of the Presidential Range (including Mount Washington), the broad Fabyan plain to the north, and the landmark Mount Washington Hotel, with its familiar fire engine red roof.

From the summit spur trail, the Avalon Trail passes over an open flat area, where a nice view of the surrounding peaks is obtained. It then continues for another mile of steep climbing to its terminus near the summit of 4,326-foot Mount Field. At its junction with the Willey Range Trail, go left (south) 100 yards to Mount Field's summit. Go right 0.9 mile to the col between Mounts Field and Tom, where the A-Z Trail intersects. Turn right here for the return trip to the Avalon Trail and the railroad depot.

Cascade Loop Trail:

This short, tenth of a mile long trail diverges left off the Avalon Trail 0.2 mile from its start. A short distance from its beginning, a sign directs hikers left 100 yards to pretty Beecher Cascade, where the waters of Crawford Brook rush through a narrow flume-like gorge. Continue along the loop trail another 150 yards to Pearl Cascade, a less spectacular, but still very picturesque spot where the brook plunges over broken ledges into a wide, round pool. The loop trail terminates in another 100 feet back on the Avalon Trail, 0.1 mile up the path from its lower loop.

Mount Tom Spur:

Beginning near the junction with the A-Z and Willey Range Trails, this short, 0.6 mile path provides the lone access to the summit of 4,047-foot Mount Tom, the northernmost 4,000-footer on the Willey Range. The Mount Tom Spur veers right (north) off the A-Z Trail in the wide, flat col between Mounts Field and Tom. It begins 0.9 mile from the start of the A-Z Trail and 2.2 miles from the railroad depot at the top of the Notch.

The spur trail climbs at moderate grades, along a rocky footway, all the way to Mount Tom's mostly wooded summit. In years past, the summit offered limited views over a small band of trees knocked over by the powerful winds which often blow across the mountaintop. The extent of the summit blowdown patch has grown considerably in recent years, however, and now the summit provides excellent vistas to the south and west. Most prominent among the distant peaks now seen from the summit are Mounts Carrigain and Hancock in the eastern Pemigewasset Wilderness, Mounts Bond and Guyot more to the north and west, and nearby Mount Field, the peak's closest southern neighbor. Good views are also had into the lush, forested Zealand Valley to the west.

On the descent, just a few hundred feet from the summit, look for an unsigned side trail (on the left) which leads 100 yards east to a fine lookout to the east and southeast. This vantage point takes in the peaks of the southern Presidential Range, the slide-scarred western slopes of Mount Webster, and the forested east ridge of Mount Field.

A-Z Trail:

This viewless path serves as a connecting trail between the Crawford Notch area and Zealand Valley region to the west. It passes over the north end of the Willey Range in the low spot (or col) between Mounts Field and Tom and terminates about a half-mile from the Appalachian Mountain Club's Zealand Falls Hut in the White Mountain National Forest.

The yellow-blazed A-Z (or Avalon-Zealand) Trail branches off the Avalon Trail 1.3 miles from its start at the Crawford Depot and Route 302. Diverging right from the Avalon Trail, the path quickly drops down into and then out of a steep gully and continues on moderate grades through an open hardwood forest, remaining well above and to the left (south) of Crawford Brook. As the trail approaches the head of the wooded ravine which separates Mount Field from Mount Tom, it descends to cross Crawford Brook, then slabs northwest up and across the headwall, finally reaching the Field-Tom col in 0.9 mile. From this point it is 0.6 mile (right) to the summit of Mount Tom via the Mount Tom Spur.

From the intersection with the Mount Tom Spur, the A-Z Trail continues straight ahead and in 100 yards meets the northern terminus of the Willey Range Trail, which leads 0.9 mile left (south) to the summit of Mount Field. The A-Z Trail descends off the ridge and col in a southwesterly direction. After a half mile or so of fairly steep downhill walking, the grade levels out and proceeds through a wet area to the U.S. Forest Service's popular Zealand Trail, where the path terminates one half-mile north of AMC's Zealand Falls Hut and 3.2 miles from the Field-Tom col.

A trail sign directs hikers around picturesque Ammonoosuc Lake at the top of Crawford Notch.

(PHOTO BY AUTHOR)

The Around-The-Lake Trail (Ammonoosuc Lake) and Red Bench Trail:

One of the Crawford Notch region's true hidden gems, Ammonoosuc Lake is a four-acre pond nestled amidst a forest of dark spruces. The lake, once a private preserve for guests at the nearby Crawford House, is reached by a pleasant mile-long loop trail which begins and ends at the site of the former grand hotel at the top of the Notch.

The trail begins at the north end of the old hotel driveway opposite the former carriage barn that is now owned by the Appalachian Mountain Club. Parking is available a tenth of a mile to the south in the main lot of AMC's Crawford Hostel. Following a sign that directs hikers left off the driveway along an old road that once provided vehicular access to the lake, the Around-The-Lake Trail veers right and enters the woods at a marked junction.

In a short distance, the loop trail splits, with the left fork circling the pond from west to east and the right fork vice versa. Bearing left from the loop junction, the trail crosses a small stream on a log bridge, then later takes a hard right and reaches Merrill Spring, a trickle of water once famous for its purity.

From the spring, the trail edges along the west shore of the lake on stone steps. Visible over the usually calm waters of the lake are the lower flanks of Mount Pierce (Clinton) to the east. On the left, up a steep embankment, are found the railroad tracks now regularly used by the Conway Scenic Railroad tourist trains.

After a short climb away from the shoreline, the Red Bench Trail leaves left. This interesting half-mile long spur continues north away from the pond and eventually crosses over the railroad tracks. On the opposite side of the tracks, it continues another few hundred yards to a scarlet wooden seat in the middle of the forest. From here is gained a unique perspective of Mount Washington and many of the peaks of the Presidential Range. It is written that 19th century Crawford House artist-in-residence Frank Shapleigh found this spot particularly endearing.

From its junction with the Red Bench Trail, the main trail continues to circle the lake in a clockwise fashion. A signed side trail at the northeast corner of the lake leads down to its north shoreline, where the best views of the lake and its surroundings are to be had, including a reflected view of Mounts Webster and Willard to the south. The main trail continues its loop from here, eventually passing a plank seat with restricted views of the pond through the trees. The plank seat is situated at the western base of an interesting geological entity known as an esker. An esker is a long, narrow ridge of sand and gravel that was once the bed of a stream that flowed beneath a glacier. When the glacial ice finally melted, left behind was this gravelly deposit. Several eskers are known to exist in the Crawford Notch-Bretton Woods area.

After passing by the plank seat, the trail soon reaches the narrow east end of the pond where its outlet flows over a small concrete dam. From the grassy opening on the south side of the dam—once the site of a bathhouse—the trail continues up the lower portion of the old road, crosses a brook, and turns right, back into the woods, reaching the loop junction in another 100 yards.

Refreshing Merrill Spring

Merrill Spring, situated on the west side of Ammonoosuc Lake and accessible by the Around-the-Lake Trail, is named for longtime Crawford House manager Cordeanio Harley (C.H.) Merrill (1840-1908). Merrill was one of the principals of the Barron, Merrill, and Barron group that operated several hotels in the area. He served as manager of the Crawford House from 1872 to 1901, taking over that position shortly after the hotel's purchase.

Merrill Spring was discovered by two hotel guests, Alvin John and Henry G. Lapham. Long noted for its purity, the spring water was made available to hotel guests from a pump-fed fountain situated in the hotel's lobby. According to hotel brochures from earlier in this century, the water from the spring maintained a refreshingly cool temperature of 40 degrees year-round. Over the years the spring has fallen into a severe state of disrepair and is no longer functioning. One must presume, however, that the water is still as fresh as once renowned.

Sam Willey Trail:

Considered one of the Crawford Notch region's easiest trails, the Sam Willey Trail provides a gentle three-quarter mile loop walk along the base of Mount Webster and beside the meandering Saco River.

Starting 150 feet from the east end of the bridge and dam over Willey Pond (directly across from the Willey House site), the trail bears right and almost immediately passes through the gravelly outwash of a slide off Mount Webster. The blue-blazed trail nears the Saco River, then steers sharp left and skirts the boulder-strewn lower slopes of Mount Webster.

At 0.3 mile, the trail splits into a loop. Staying to the left, the trail continues along the base of the mountain, then gradually curves right where it meets the Saco River at a sandy clearing. Maintaining its course on the east side of the river, the trail continues through the woods and passes several short side paths leading to the Saco River's shoreline. At a point where the trail veers away from the river, good views are obtained of the upper slopes of Mount Webster. From here the trail continues a short distance more and ends back at the loop intersection.

Pond Loop Trail:

This short trail across from the Willey House site on Route 302 provides an easy quarter-mile loop hike along the east shore of Willey Pond and in the woods at the base of slide-scarred Mount Webster.

Cross the bridge and dam at the south end of Willey Pond and continue straight ahead for 150 feet to a point where a sign directs hikers to go left for the pond loop. Passing over a graded path in an area where the state formerly operated a summertime animal preserve, the trail skirts the base of Mount Webster for 100 yards, then reaches a short side path to the left which leads in 50 feet to a large boulder with an interesting overhang.

The trail then circles to the left and reaches the east shore of the pond where nice views are obtained of Mounts Willard, Avalon and Field. After passing by several shoreline picnic areas, the trail terminates at the east end of the bridge and dam.

(Both the Sam Willey Trail and Pond Loop Trail have been designated as the Ethan Allen Crawford Nature Trails).

Kedron Flume Trail:

This 1.3-mile long trail, first opened in 1936, connects the Willey House site in Crawford Notch with the Ethan Pond Trail. The lower portion of this path is easy with moderate grades, while the upper half of the trail is much rougher and steeper. The path begins behind the snack bar and gift shop and in 0.4 mile crosses the now active railroad line. Kedron Flume, an interesting cascade on Kedron Brook, is reached in 1.0 mile. The grade from here to Ethan Pond Trail is significantly steeper. Kedron Flume Trail terminates at the Ethan Pond Trail 1.3 miles from its start off Route 302 and 0.3 mile from the southern terminus of the Willey Range Trail.

Willey Range Trail:

This steep, rugged trail traverses two of the three 4,000-foot summits along the Willey Range, which forms the western wall to Crawford Notch. It runs nearly three and a half miles from the southern base of Mount Willey to the col between Mounts Field and Tom.

The southern end of the trail is accessed by the Ethan Pond Trail, which starts at the site of the former Willey House Station at the end of a short paved road off Route 302, a mile south of the Willey House site and directly across from the Webster Cliff Trail (and Appalachian Trail).

The Ethan Pond Trail is followed for 1.6 miles. At the point where it turns left to go up and over the height-of-land toward Ethan Pond, the Willey Range Trail continues straight ahead. After a crossing of Kedron Brook, the trail continues on easy to moderate grades for 0.4 mile before it begins the unrelievedly steep ascent of Mount Willey's south slopes. Wooden ladders provide assistance over the steepest ledges.

The best views from Mount Willey's summit area are found by following an unsigned foot path to the right approximately 40 yards below the summit. Here there is a spectacular panorama of the Presidential Range, the Webster Cliffs, Crawford Notch, and many distant mountains to the east and south. Views are also obtained from another lookout a short distance past the summit, where there is a sweeping vista over the expansive eastern region of the Pemigewasset Wilderness.

The trail continues north 1.5 miles at easy to moderate grades along the ridgecrest from Willey's 4,302-foot summit to the top of Mount Field (4,326 feet), high point of the Willey Range. Limited views to the south and west are obtained over summit trees. A short side trail to the right of the summit cairn offers an outstanding view to the north, with the grand Mount Washington Hotel and its namesake mountain the centerpieces of the outlook vista.

From the summit of Mount Field, the trail passes by in 100 yards the ridgetop terminus of the Avalon Trail, which leads in 2.6 miles to Crawford Depot. Descending on easy grades from this junction, the Willey Range Trail steers to the northwest and eventually winds up in the col between Mounts Tom and Field, where it terminates at its junction with the A-Z Trail. From here it is 2.3 miles right (east) to Crawford's, 3.4 miles back to the Ethan Pond Trail, 5.0 miles from the Ethan Pond trailhead, and 3.2 miles west to the Zealand Trail near Zealand Falls.

Bog bridges are laid out across a wet area of the Webster Cliff Trail between Mount Jackson (seen in background) and Mizpah Spring Hut.
(PHOTO BY AUTHOR)

Webster Cliff Trail:

Running a total of 7.3 miles from Route 302 (a mile south of the Willey House site) to its terminus a short distance north of Mount Pierce's (Clinton) summit, this spectacular but unheralded trail provides outstanding vistas from numerous areas along the ridgeline running north to Mount Washington.

A link in the Appalachian Trail, the Webster Cliff Trail passes over three summits with elevations at or approaching 4,000 feet. The section of trail passing along the ridge just south of 3,910-foot Mount Webster–the eastern wall of Crawford Notch–is particularly attractive as a series of outlook ledges offer stunning views of the floor of the Notch and much of the surrounding mountain terrain.

The trail, blazed with white rectangles, begins off Route 302 across from the access road to the former Willey House Station. Beginning on the east side of the highway, the trail crosses the Saco River on a bridge in 0.1 mile, then heads east on easy to moderate grades before beginning a grueling ascent of Mount Webster's southern slopes.

The first outlook is reached in 1.8 miles. Numerous others are passed in the next 1.5 miles as the trail grinds its way north to Webster's true summit.

After passing the Webster branch of the Webster-Jackson Trail in another 0.1 mile, the trail veers northeast and passes through a wet area before reaching the ledgy cone of Mount Jackson in 4.7 miles. Continuing almost due north, the trail passes through an alpine meadow on its way to AMC's Mizpah Spring Hut, reached in 1.7 miles (or 6.4 miles from Route 302).

Leaving the hut, the trail climbs steeply at first, soon reaching a ledge with views back toward Mount Jackson. It then proceeds over the southwest knob of Mount Pierce, drops into a slight sag, then climbs to the 4,310-foot main summit. The trail ends 150 yards northeast of the summit at the point where the Crawford Path enters left from Route 302.

Ethan Pond Trail:

A link in the 2,160-mile Appalachian Trail, the Ethan Pond Trail runs 7.4 miles from the old Willey House Station site to the Zealand Falls area. At 2.6 miles, it passes nearby remote Ethan Pond, a five-acre backcountry tarn named after pioneer innkeeper Ethan Allen Crawford. Ethan Pond, situated at the western base

The waters of Ethan Pond as seen from its southern shoreline.
(PHOTO BY STEVE SMITH)

of Mount Willey, is considered the source of the Merrimack River.

The white-blazed trail starts near the Willey House Station site at the end of the 0.3 mile long paved road west off Route 302, a mile south of the Willey House site. Initially it coincides with the Ripley Falls Trail, but after just 0.2 mile, it veers right away from the falls and begins a steep, then more steady climb along an old logging road. At 1.3 miles, the Kedron Flume Trail from the Willey House enters right, and in 1.6 miles the Ethan Pond Trail turns left while the Willey Range Trail goes straight ahead along the ridge.

After passing over the height-of-land, the trail leaves the state park and enters the White Mountain National Forest. It soon picks up an old logging road and at 2.6 miles meets a short side path to the right which leads to a nice lookout towards the Twin-Bond Range at the southeast corner of Ethan Pond. AMC maintains a shelter and several tentsites here for overnight campers. From the pond, the trail continues north–passing by spur trails to remote Shoal Pond and Thoreau Falls–following for much of the way the grade of J.E. Henry's late 19th century Zealand Valley logging railroad. After passing through spectacular Zealand Notch and the base of Whitewall Mountain, the trail ends 4.8 miles from

Ethan Pond at the intersection of the Zealand and Twinway Trails near Zealand Falls.

Ripley Falls Trail:

One of the most popular family hikes in Crawford Notch, this half-mile walk leads from the former Willey House Station site to the base of 100-foot high Ripley Falls on Avalanche Brook. It coincides with the Ethan Pond Trail for the first 0.2 mile, then diverges left and slabs a hillside for 0.3 mile before dropping down to the base of the waterfall. A 2.5-mile connecting trail, the Arethusa-Ripley Falls Trail (see below), links Ripley Falls with its sister Crawford Notch waterfall to the south. Parking for this trail is at the end of the short paved road to the east, one mile south of the Willey House site.

Arethusa Falls Trail:

This trail near the south entrance to the state park leads in 1.3 miles to Arethusa Falls, reputedly the highest waterfall in New Hampshire, with a drop approaching 200 feet. Following old woods roads and generally the course of Bemis Brook, the trail rises by moderate grades on a somewhat rough and rocky path until reaching the base of the falls.

The blue-blazed trail begins off Route 302 at a large parking area 0.5 mile south of Dry River Campground. A short paved road leads uphill from the highway to a railroad crossing and private home, where the path leaves left into the woods.

Hikers headed to the falls may choose to follow the course of the Bemis Brook Trail (see below), a side path that parallels the main route, but a bit closer to its namesake brook. The Arethusa-Ripley Falls Trail (also see below), meanwhile, begins its 2.5 mile course at the base of Arethusa Falls.

A rough, rooty side trail to the top of the falls may be followed for 0.1 mile. This footpath is found at the base of the falls on the left side. Persons climbing to the ledges atop the falls should use extreme caution once above the falls as the rocks tend to be wet and slippery. Several hikers have lost their lives in accidental falls from the top, including one as recently as 1995.

Bemis Brook Trail:

This half-mile long trail provides an attractive alternate route for trampers heading to or from Arethusa Falls. It leaves the

A hiker sits at the base of scenic Ripley Falls, one of the more popular hiking destinations for Crawford Notch visitors.

(PHOTO BY AUTHOR)

Arethusa Falls Trail 0.1 mile from its beginning and soon reaches the north side of Bemis Brook. Proceeding on mostly easy grades, the trail passes by three notable spots along the brook—Fawn Pool, Bemis Falls, and Coliseum Falls. From Coliseum Falls, the trail diverges right for the steep climb back up to the Arethusa Falls Trail, rejoining it approximately a half-mile from its start.

Arethusa-Ripley Falls Trail:

Traversing the high plateau behind Frankenstein Cliff, this trail connects the park's two highest waterfalls via a 2.5-mile long path. Sections of this trail are infamous for being partially blocked by windblown trees, despite yearly efforts by state parks personnel to clear the footpath of the blowdowns.

The north end of the trail begins at the base of Ripley Falls, on the south side of Avalanche Brook. Following a moderately steep climb of about a half-mile, the trail levels out and wanders along the ridge at easy grades until reaching the junction of the Frankenstein Cliff Trail at 1.2 miles. The main trail steers right (west), then gradually slabs more south to Bemis Brook and the base of Arethusa Falls.

In the opposite direction, the trail begins at the upper end of the Arethusa Falls Trail. After crossing Bemis Brook, the trail angles up and away from the falls and eventually turns more to the east. At 1.3 miles, the Frankenstein Cliff Trail enters (right). After a lengthy stretch of level walking on the ridge, the trail begins its descent to Ripley Falls via a series of switchbacks. A spur trail to the left leads to the top of the falls. A rough trail to the south of the waterfall leads to its base and the northern terminus of the Arethusa-Ripley Trail.

As the rocks at the top of the waterfall tend to be extremely slick, especially in times of wet weather, it is advisable to avoid them or risk a fall and possible injury.

Frankenstein Cliff Trail:

The primary access route to the prominent series of cliffs and ledges seen best from Route 302 in the vicinity of Dry River Campground, this rugged trail leads in 1.3 miles to a spectacular outlook providing a unique perspective on the southern area of the Crawford Notch region. It begins near the Arethusa Falls trailhead and terminates in 2.1 miles at its junction with the Arethusa-Ripley Falls Trail.

The trail begins off either of the two parking areas situated on the paved Arethusa Falls Road, which lies just a few hundred yards north of the state park highway sign. From the small lot at the upper end of the road (near the railroad tracks), the trail heads off into the woods on the right (signed). From the newer and larger dirt parking area at the bottom of the road, just off Route 302, a signboard at the north end of the lot directs hikers into the woods on a green-blazed connecting trail which links up with the upper trail in 0.1 mile.

Staying roughly parallel to, but well below the grade of the railroad tracks, the path continues one half-mile over rough terrain to a point where the original Frankenstein Cliff Trail from Route 302 entered on the right. The trail goes left here, and soon passes under the famous Frankenstein railroad trestle. Ascending steeply, mainly by switchbacks, the trail then makes its way up to the main ridge, skirting to the north of the cliffs, and then finally reaching its main outlook in 1.3 miles. From the outlook, the path continues in a northwesterly direction to the ridgetop summit, where some additional views are obtained. As the trail reaches the height-of-land, it levels off and continues on to its junction with the Arethusa-Ripley Falls Trail.

With the start-up of a tourist train operation through Crawford Notch in 1995, travel along the railroad tracks and trestle is dangerous in the summer months, when trains run daily. Be aware of the train schedule and also the possibility that work crews may be traveling along the railroad line any time from mid-April to late November. Some ledges just past the north end of the trestle provide an excellent viewpoint for persons wishing to watch the train as it passes over the century-old steel landmark.

Davis Path:

Originally constructed as a bridle path in 1844 by Nathaniel P.T. Davis, this trail is one of the oldest and longest in the White Mountains. It runs 14.4 miles from its start at the south end of the Notch all the way to the upper end of the Crawford Path, just 0.6 mile from Mount Washington's 6,288-foot summit.

The trailhead is situated on the east side of Route 302 across the highway from the Notchland Inn. The large paved parking lot at the trailhead is 5.6 miles south of the Willey House site and a couple miles outside the state park boundary.

The suspension bridge over the Saco River at the south end of the Notch marks the start of the Davis Path, which leads in 15 miles to the summit of Mount Washington.

(PHOTO BY AUTHOR)

The Davis Path crosses over the Saco River on a suspension bridge, briefly passes over private land, then joins an old woods road. After a short, level stretch, the trail begins a steep and rough two-mile climb towards Mount Crawford. At 2.2 miles, a side trail leading in 0.3 mile to the bare summit of Mount Crawford diverges left. The rocky summit of Mount Crawford provides one of the finest views in the White Mountains, with a unique southern perspective on Crawford Notch and the Presidential Range.

The main path continues its course to the northeast, passing by the ledgy shoulder of Crawford Dome and then slabbing the west slope of Mount Resolution. At 3.7 miles, the Mount Parker Trail enters on the right, while to the left, a short, steep side path leads down to AMC's Resolution Shelter—a log lean-to accommodating eight overnight campers.

Beyond the shelter, the trail climbs the back (or southwest) side of Stairs Mountain. The Stairs Col Trail from the Rocky Branch valley is met at 4.0 miles, while a spur path to an open viewpoint at the top of the Giant Stairs is attained in 4.4 miles.

The trail continues north from here along the Montalban Ridge, passing near the summits of Mount Davis (3,840 feet) and Mount Isolation (4,005 feet). Both summits offer outstanding views and are accessible by short spur trails off the Davis Path. The spur trail to Mount Davis is reached in 8.7 miles while the Mount Isolation spur path is reached in 9.7 miles.

From Isolation, the trail continues its northward advance toward Mount Washington. After passing by both the east and west branches of the connecting Isolation Trail, the Davis Path climbs steadily and reaches treeline at 12.1 miles. The Glen Boulder Trail from Pinkham Notch joins in on the right at 12.5 miles, while the summit of Boott Spur (5,500 feet) is reached at the 13.0 mile mark.

Turning northwest from here, the trail crosses exposed, flat Bigelow Lawn, just below Washington's summit cone. It meets up with the Crawford Path in 14.4 miles and continues another 0.6 mile to the summit of the northeast's highest peak.

Much of the Davis Path passes through the Presidential Range-Dry River Wilderness. Camping and fires are not allowed above treeline (or where trees are not at least eight feet tall), except where snow is two or more feet deep. Camping within 200 feet of any trail is also prohibited, except at designated sites. Federal wilderness regulations also prohibit camping groups of 10 or more persons.

Dry River Trail:

This rugged footpath into the Presidential Range-Dry River Wilderness provides a connecting trail from the south end of Crawford Notch State Park to AMC's Lakes of the Clouds Hut at the southwest base of Mount Washington.

The first half of this 9.6 mile trail follows closely a century-old logging railroad grade, while the latter half of the trail passes through the remote, wild surroundings of the upper Dry River valley and spectacular Oakes Gulf.

The trail begins off Route 302 at a point 0.4 mile north of the state-run Dry River Campground. In its first 6.5 miles, several crossings of the Dry River (or Mount Washington River as it is also known) are required. These crossings can be extremely hazardous in times of high water and several hikers over the years have drowned in accidents along the river. The first crossing, 1.7 miles into the hike, is on a suspension bridge that brings hikers to the east side of the river. The next major crossing is at 5.6 miles, while the third crossing, this time over a major tributary of the Dry River, is reached at 6.4 miles.

Grades are easy for the first mile, with a path from Dry River Campground joining from the right at 0.5 mile. At 1.6 miles a short, steep climb leads to a beautiful tree-framed outlook up the valley towards Mount Washington, making this a nice objective for a short hike.

At the 2.9 mile mark, the Mount Clinton Trail to AMC's Mizpah Spring Hut diverges left, while the Isolation Trail to the upper end of Montalban Ridge diverges right at 4.9 miles. The Mount Eisenhower Trail, which links with the Crawford Path just north of Mount Eisenhower, diverges left and crosses the river at 5.2 miles.

The scenic Dry River Falls, accessed by a short side trail to the left, are passed at 5.4 miles. Dry River Shelter No. 3, the only remaining lean-to in the valley, is reached at 6.3 miles.

At 7.4 miles the trail finally diverges away from the stream and begins its climb into Oakes Gulf–a great glacial cirque south of Mount Washington's summit cone. The trail gets rougher and steeper as it begins to ascend the headwall of Oakes Gulf. Emerging out of the scrub at 8.7 miles, magnificent views back down the Dry River valley are obtained.

After reaching the lip of the headwall at 9.1 miles, the trail cuts sharp right, away from its former route through an area of endangered alpine flowers. It then passes out of the designated wilderness area, crosses over a height-of-land, and descends in 0.2 mile to Lakes of the Clouds and the Crawford Path.

Logging the Dry River Valley

The Saco Valley Railroad, incorporated on April 7, 1891, conducted logging operations for a five and a half year period beginning in 1892 and ending in 1898. Despite its name, the company concentrated its efforts in the virgin forests of the valley of the Mount Washington River, or Dry River as it is known today.

The logging railroad operated in an area considered amongst the toughest and most inaccessible ever tackled by White Mountain lumberjacks. In its course up the narrow, V-shaped valley leading up to rugged Oakes Gulf, the railroad crossed the river 13 times in a four-mile span. The trestles over which the trains crossed the river were quite vulnerable to the ravages of the river, which has long been among the fiercest in the region in times of high water. Just nine years after logging operations concluded on the Saco River Railroad, every one of the trestles had been swept away by floodwaters.

The timber operations in the Dry River valley are heralded today as being among the most conservation-minded of the times. Under the cutting agreement entered into between the land owners—the Cutts family of Saco, Maine and the Conant family of Portland, Maine—the Saco Valley Lumber Company, which had cutting rights to the stumpage, could only remove trees eight inches or more in diameter at the stump, and they had to complete the job in a 15-year time span. As a result of this unique timber contract, the Dry River valley was able to regenerate itself in a relatively short period of time, even though the lumberjacks reportedly cut between 11 and 12 million board feet of timber from the valley each year of its limited operation.

Nancy Pond Trail:

The southernmost of the hiking trails considered a part of the Crawford Notch region, this trail leads to the shallow mountain tarns, Nancy and Norcross Ponds, both situated within the boundary of the White Mountain National Forest.

The Nancy Pond Trail leaves the west side of Route 302 approximately 3.5 miles south of the Crawford Notch State Park border, and one mile south of the Davis Path parking area. The yellow-blazed path follows old logging roads for the first 2.4 miles, or until it reaches the base of the scenic Nancy Cascades. At 1.8 miles, a short distance after crossing over boulder-strewn Nancy Brook, look to your left for the remains of an old mill used for timber salvage after the Hurricane of 1938.

Climbing over steep terrain via switchbacks, the trail ascends to the top of the cascades (on your right). Views of the middle cascade and the mountain summits across the valley to the east are obtained from certain vantage points along the trail.

At 2.8 miles the trail levels out and passes through a stunningly beautiful stand of virgin conifers—one of the largest such stands in all of New England. At 3.4 miles the northeast shore of swampy Nancy Pond is reached, while Norcross Pond, the larger and more open of the two backcountry ponds, is reached in another 10 minutes of walking. Between the ponds you enter the Pemigewasset Wilderness. From the outlet of Norcross Pond (4.3 miles) at its northwest shore, the trail continues west an additional 2.8 miles to its terminus at the Carrigain Notch Trail.

The two mountain ponds accessed by the trail provide excellent habitat for a number of unusual or rare birds of the northern boreal forest. A set of ledges near the outlet of Norcross Pond, meanwhile, provide a unique perspective on the distant peaks of the Twin-Bond Range across the eastern Pemi Wilderness.

Hiking Tips

Here are a few pointers to ensure a safe and enjoyable hike in the Crawford Notch area:

- Choose a hike suited to the interests, abilities and fitness of your group. The accompanying list of hikes suggests easy, moderate, and more difficult outings. Plan your route using a good guidebook or map such as the *AMC White Mountain*

Guide or the Wilderness Map Company's Crawford Notch map. Allow ample time to complete your trek, remembering that both distance and vertical rise figure into the difficulty. And leave word of your itinerary with family or friends.

– Know the weather forecast before setting out. Recorded local forecasts are available by calling 444-2656 (Littleton) or 447-5252 (Conway), or call the Appalachian Mountain Club's Pinkham Notch Camp at 466-2727. Weather can change very rapidly in the White Mountains. If the weather goes bad, turn back before your group gets wet, cold and potentially hypothermic. This is especially important on the higher ridges.

– Wear sturdy, broken-in footgear. Sneakers may be okay on some of the easier hikes, but good hiking boots are essential on the rougher mountain trails.

– Dress in loose-fitting, comfortable clothing suitable for the season and elevation of the hike. In cooler weather use the layering system to regulate body temperature. Wool and synthetics such as polypropylene are much better than cotton for warmth and insulation, especially when wet.

– Bring a day pack with the essentials: extra clothing, rain and wind gear, plenty of food and water, map/guidebook and compass, bug dope, first aid kit, toilet paper, flashlight, pocket knife, matches and sunglasses. If you're venturing to one of the higher summits, bring a warm jacket, long pants, winter hat and gloves. Wintry weather can occur at any time of year up high and is especially dangerous above treeline on the Crawford Path beyond Mount Pierce.

– Set a steady, moderate pace on the trail. Watch your footing carefully on rocky and rooty sections, especially when wet, and also at stream crossings. Keep your group together and always wait up at trail junctions so no one goes astray.

– Take care to minimize your impact on the fragile mountain environment, preserving it for future visitors to enjoy. Carry out what you carry in and bring out any litter you find. Please stay on the footway and avoid widening muddy spots or trampling sensitive vegetation. This is especially important above treeline, where careless steps can kill rare plants. The call of nature should be answered at least 200 feet from any stream, pond or trail, and waste should be buried in a cat hole six to eight inches deep. Please don't pick wildflowers or disturb wildlife. Also, authorities request that hikers avoid wet, erodible trails during the "mud season" of April and May.

– Most of all, enjoy your hike, the company of family or friends, and the beautiful natural world that surrounds you in Crawford Notch!

Rating the Hikes

(Round-trip distance is given in miles, total vertical ascent is given in feet.)

Easy Hikes

Sam Willey Trail: 0.8 mile, no climbing.

Elephant Head: 0.6 mile, 150 feet on Webster-Jackson Trail and Elephant Head Spur.

Gibbs Falls: 0.8 mile, 200 feet on Crawford Path.

Saco Lake: 0.5 mile, no climbing on Saco Lake Trail.

Ripley Falls: 1.2 mile, 350 feet on Ethan Pond Trail and Ripley Falls Trail.

Ammonoosuc Lake: 1.0 mile, 75 feet on Around-the-Lake Trail. Add 1.0 mile, 100 feet for side trip to Red Bench viewpoint.

Bugle Cliff: 1.2 mile, 500 feet on Webster-Jackson Trail.

Moderate Hikes

Dry River Outlook: 3.2 miles, 500 feet on Dry River Trail.

Frankenstein Cliff: 2.6 miles, 1,000 feet on Frankenstein Cliff Trail.

Arethusa Falls: 2.6 miles, 900 feet on Arethusa Falls Trail.

Mount Willard: 3.2 miles, 950 feet on Mount Willard Trail.

Mount Avalon: 3.8 miles, 1,500 feet on Avalon Trail.

Ethan Pond: 5.5 miles, 1,600 feet on Ethan Pond Trail.

Nancy Cascades: 4.8 miles, 1,500 feet on Nancy Pond Trail.

More Difficult Hikes

Mount Jackson: 5.2 miles, 2,150 feet on Webster-Jackson Trail. Loop over Mount Webster via Webster Cliff Trail and Webster branch of Webster-Jackson Trail: 6.5 miles, 2,350 feet.

Mount Crawford: 5.0 miles, 2,100 feet on Davis Path and

Mount Crawford Spur. Continuing to Giant Stairs on Davis Path and spur: 9.8 miles, 2,700 feet.

Mount Pierce: 6.0 miles, 2,400 feet on Crawford Path and Webster Cliff Trail. Loop back via Webster Cliff Trail and Mizpah Cut-Off: 6.2 miles, 2,500 feet.

Webster Cliffs and Mount Webster: 6.6 miles, 2,650 feet on Webster Cliff Trail.

Mounts Field and Willey: 8.4 miles, 3,100 feet on Avalon Trail and Willey Range Trail.

Nancy and Norcross Ponds: 8.6 miles, 2,200 feet on Nancy Pond Trail.

Dry River Falls: 10.8 miles, 1,600 feet on Dry River Trail.

FOURTEEN

Winter Activities in the Notch

While the Crawford Notch area sees the bulk of its visitors during the warmer months of the year—generally Memorial Day through Columbus Day—it is by no means abandoned during the cold months of winter. Increasing numbers of outdoor enthusiasts are finding their way to the White Mountains each year, and since Crawford Notch offers a variety of activities for the most intrepid skiers, snowshoers, and ice climbers, it has turned into a popular winter recreation playground.

Hiking is certainly a year-round sport in the White Mountains, and with its abundance of trails, Crawford Notch lures its share of winter hikers and snowshoers to the area even in the coldest and snowiest times of the year. Just as in the summer and fall months, the trek up Mount Willard is a major draw in winter. So are the Crawford Path up onto the Presidential Range, the Willey Range Trail over Mounts Field and Willey, and the Ethan Pond Trail to Ethan Pond.

With one of the East's largest touring centers just a few miles away at Bretton Woods, cross country ski enthusiasts frequently pass through and/or visit Crawford Notch. Bretton Woods Ski Area offers approximately 100 kilometers of skiing on groomed trails, many of them situated in the White Mountain National Forest. The extensive network of trails extends almost all the way to the top of the Notch, while some ski trails also climb the slopes of the Rosebrook Range, a few miles north of Mount Tom and the northern end of the Willey Range. The Appalachian Mountain Club also runs several cross country skiing (or snowshoeing) workshops out of its Crawford Notch Hostel at the top of the Notch.

The Crawford Notch area is also known for its superb ice climbing venues. The most popular ice climbing areas are found on the east face of Mount Willey, the south face of Mount Willard,

An ice climber works his way up a slab on Mount Willard.

(PHOTO BY BILL FLYNN)

on the Frankenstein Cliffs in the southern reaches of the state park, and up remote Arethusa Falls.

Motorists passing through the Notch on Route 302 can frequently spot climbers inching their way up the frozen slabs of water on Willey's Slide, located on the lower east face of Mount Willey. This is one of the most visited ice climbing areas on the

Winter hikers march their way up the Crawford Path on the way to Mount Pierce, a peak in the southern Presidential Range.

(PHOTO BY AUTHOR)

East Coast. Parking for climbers headed for Willey's Slide is provided at two dirt pullouts a half-mile north of the Willey House site.

Across the way on Mount Webster, ice climbers are challenged by some of the longest climbs in the region along the mountain's famous alpine gullies. With an elevation gain of some 2,500 feet, these gullies can be especially challenging to ice climbers used to shorter routes and ascents. The most popular ice climbing routes on Mount Webster are known as Shoestring Gully, Landslide Gully, and Horseshoe Gully.

Frankenstein Cliff offers probably the greatest variety of ice climbing routes of any place in Crawford Notch. Its most popular routes include Fang, First Ascent Gully and Young Frankenstein.

Mounts Bemis, Avalon and Tom, along with the Elephant Head near the Gateway, also offer limited climbing opportunities in winter.

For detailed descriptions of ice climbing routes in Crawford Notch, consult *An Ice Climber's Guide to Northern New England* by Rick Wilcox.

FIFTEEN

Nomenclature of Crawford Notch

AMMONOOSUC LAKE, Ammonoosuc River

Formerly the private preserve of guests at the luxurious Crawford House, this four-acre pond nestled in the spruce woods between the railroad and the highway is a gem that generally receives a scant amount of attention when compared to other natural features of the Crawford Notch region.

Surrounded as it is by White Mountain National Forest land, and invisible to visitors passing through the area along busy Route 302, the setting along its shoreline is serene and unusually quiet. The view from its northern shore, with Mounts Webster and Willard providing the dramatic backdrop, is one of the most pleasant to be found in the area.

The pond gets its name from the river into which its waters flow—the Ammonoosuc River (from the Abenaki language, "fish place"). Unlike nearby Saco Lake, which is the headwaters for the Saco River which flows eastward to the Atlantic Ocean and the Maine coast, Ammonoosuc Lake drains north and west towards Bretton Woods, through which its namesake river passes after forming high up on the western slopes of Mount Washington in the Lakes of the Clouds.

AVALANCHE BROOK:

Once known as Cow Brook, this mountain stream flows off the ridgeline just south of Mount Willey, not far from the scene of the tragic 1826 landslide that killed the Willey family in Crawford

Notch. Nineteenth century writer Rev. Thomas Starr King and his good friend, Henry Wheeler Ripley, are credited with renaming the stream in remembrance of the Willey tragedy. Guidebook author Moses Sweetser, in the latter part of the 19th century, noted, however, that the stream still retained its original "homely" name as late as 1892. Avalanche Brook is one of the Crawford Notch region's most visited streams as the scenic Ripley Falls tumble off the mountainside just a half-mile walk in from the railroad tracks near the old Willey House Station site.

AVALON, MOUNT:

White Mountain guidebook author Moses Sweetser bestowed the name on this sharp, 3,430-foot peak back in the latter part of the 19th century. He likened the mountain to the Hills of Avalon in Newfoundland. This spur peak of Mount Field, with its rocky open summit, offers hikers one of the finest views of the Notch and the nearby southern peaks of the Presidential Range.

ARETHUSA FALLS:

This spectacular 200-foot high waterfall on Bemis Brook was first discovered by noted 19th century botanist Dr. Edward Tuckerman, sometime around 1840. The falls were seldom visited, and remained nameless until 1875, when guidebook author Moses Sweetser and assistant state geologist J.H. Huntington paid a visit to the "well nigh" forgotten falls. The name they chose for the waterfall alludes to a poem of the same name by Percy Bysshe Shelley. The poem tells the Greek myth of a beautiful nymph who is transformed into a fountain.

The falls themselves and the land surrounding them became the property of the state of New Hampshire in 1930, when 25 acres of forest land on each side of Bemis Brook were acquired from descendants of the Saunders brothers, who for years operated a lumbering business in Livermore and along the Sawyer River valley, several miles south of the Notch. The purchase was

---

OPPOSITE PAGE: *In years past, guests at the nearby Crawford House used the waters of Ammonoosuc Lake to refresh themselves during the dog days of summer. The above photo is taken from the north shore of the pond, looking south toward Mount Willard and Mount Webster.*
(AUTHOR'S COLLECTION)

Sheets of water tumble over the rocks that form 200-foot high Arethusa Falls, highest waterfall in the state.

(PHOTO BY AUTHOR)

made possible through the efforts of Mary Peabody Williamson of Cleveland, Ohio, an AMC member and longtime patron of the Crawford House who "offered to furnish the funds necessary to acquire the property" according to an article in the June 1931 issue of AMC's *Appalachia* journal.

BEECHER CASCADE:

This series of scenic waterfalls along Crawford Brook at the top of the Notch are named for Henry Ward Beecher (1813-1887), the Brooklyn, N.Y. clergyman, author and lecturer who summered annually in nearby Twin Mountain. Beecher not only loved to explore the White Mountains and their natural wonders, but also gave stirring Sunday sermons each week from under a tent set up near the Twin Mountain House. It was here, one 19th century writer wrote, that Beecher, "expounded broad-church Congregationalism and Christian liberality to all who could assemble in the great tent." Like many early summer visitors to the region, Beecher escaped to the White Mountains to seek respite from hay fever, which afflicted him for up to six weeks each year. As Frederick W. Kilbourne noted in his classic history of the region, *Chronicles of the White Mountains*, Beecher "happily found exemption there from the attacks of the disease."

In Beecher's later years of life, he was involved in a scandalous adultery trial in which he was accused of having had an affair with the wife of a longtime friend and writing colleague. The sensational 1875 trial ended with a hung jury, six months after it began. Beecher was also cleared of the adultery charges by a council of Congregational churches.

BEMIS BROOK, Bemis Ridge, and Mount Bemis:

All three Crawford Notch landmarks are named for Dr. Samuel Bemis, a Boston dentist who frequented the Crawford Notch region in the early 1800s and eventually built the stone house (now known as the Notchland Inn) in the southern reaches of the Notch. He acquired Abel Crawford's extensive land holdings in the Notch through foreclosure shortly after the elder Crawford's death in 1851 and eventually became known locally as the "Lord of the Valley."

Bemis was also an early photography buff, and was among one of the few Americans of his day to own a daguerreotype camera—imported from Europe—which he used to photograph

Samuel Bemis, the mid-19th century "Lord of the Valley," is immortal-ized in this painting which hangs in the parlor of the Notchland Inn.
(PHOTO BY AUTHOR)

some of the area's earliest buildings, such as Crawford's old tavern.

Described as an enthusiastic explorer of the mountains, Bemis was responsible for the naming of several area natural landmarks, such as the Giant Stairs, Mount Crawford, and Mount Resolution.

Bemis Brook flows into the Saco River a short distance south of the state park entrance near Frankenstein Cliffs. The most famous feature of the brook is 200-foot high Arethusa Falls. Mount Bemis is a thickly wooded 3,706-foot mountain several miles to the south of Bemis Brook. From 1940-48, the U.S. Forest Service manned a fire lookout's tower from the summit, the remains of which are still evident to adventurous hikers making their way to the wooded mountaintop. Bemis Ridge is situated on the east side of Route 302 at the south end of the Notch and includes the peaks of Mount Crawford (3,129 feet) and Mount Hope (2,520 feet).

BUGLE CLIFF

An interesting and expansive ledge situated on the lower western flanks of Mount Jackson, Bugle Cliff (at 2,500 feet elevation) offers superb views of Crawford Notch and the region just above the Gateway. The cliff is reached via a spur path along the Webster-Jackson Trail, 0.6 mile from its start. To reach the ledge, descend from the trail a couple hundred feet to the rocky perch well above the highway below. Use extreme caution here, particularly when conditions are wet and slippery.

One can only speculate how this prominent ledge got its name. Perhaps a patron at the old Crawford House once entertained fellow guests with a tune or two played from this lofty perch.

BUTTERWORT FLUME

The lesser known of Mount Willard's two narrow gorges, Butterwort Flume was discovered by state geologist Charles Hitchcock during his exhaustive state geological study of the 1870s. It is named for the beautiful flower *Pinguicula vulgaris*, or Butterwort, which Hitchcock found growing in it at the time of its discovery.

The flume is situated south of its sister gorge, Hitchcock Flume, and is divided into two sections—an upper and lower. Hitchcock reported in 1877 that, "As one stands on the slope of Mt. Webster, or even at the bottom of the steep hill in the Notch, and looks up at Mt. Willard, he can see this flume extending downwards for perhaps 500 feet of vertical ascent, or pointing directly towards a blacksmith's shop on the railroad, about 3000 feet north of Willey Brook." Unlike Hitchcock Flume, there are no walking or hiking trails to this gorge.

COLISEUM FALLS

A two-tiered waterfall along Bemis Brook, less than a quarter-mile from its eastern terminus on the Arethusa Falls Trail, Coliseum Falls resembles a miniature amphitheater when viewed from the brook's shoreline. The falls are reached by the Bemis Brook Trail and can be found about 75 yards upstream from Fawn Pool, a delightful little pool reached by a short side path off the main trail.

Coliseum Falls' uppermost fall cascades over a series of step-like granite slabs. After passing a larger, level slab, the brook continues over a series of horizontal rock shelves from which the waterfall has gained its name. The falls are reached either by a spur path off the Bemis Brook Trail, or by following the streambed up from Fawn Pool.

CRAWFORD NOTCH, Mount Crawford,
Crawford Cliff:

Once known simply as the Notch of the White Mountains, Crawford Notch (and other local landmarks) now bears the name of the family that first brought mountain hospitality to the region just west of Mount Washington. Family patriarch Abel Crawford and his wife, Hannah (Rosebrook) Crawford, first settled in the area in 1792. Along with their brood of eight sons and one daughter, the Crawfords developed several of the first overnight accommodations for travelers in the Notch area and were instrumental in constructing some of the earliest trails up to then rarely explored Mount Washington. Ethan Allen Crawford, the second son to be born to Abel and his wife, is certainly the best known of the Crawford clan. His hunting, fishing, and mountain guiding experiences are legendary in nature and were related best in the classic book, *History of the White Mountains* by Lucy Crawford, Ethan's wife. Another of the Crawfords, Tom, managed an early hotel near the Gateway to the Notch.

Mount Crawford, a bare, rocky 3,129-foot peak, is the culminating point of Bemis Ridge, a north-to-south running mountain ridge lying east of the Saco River between Bartlett and Crawford Notch. The summit, from which excellent views toward Mount Washington are obtained, is reached via a spur path off the Davis Path.

Crawford Cliff (also once known as Eagle Cliff or the Eagle's Nest) is a ledgy outlook on the lower western slopes of Mount Pierce (Clinton) overlooking the former Crawford House site at the top of the Notch.. A side trail off the Crawford Connector trail is used to reach this rarely visited viewpoint.

DAVIS, MOUNT, Davis Path, Davis Brook:

The three Crawford Notch landmarks bearing the Davis name are in recognition of Nathaniel T. P. Davis, the husband of Hannah Crawford, who was the lone daughter of Abel Crawford. For a number of years Davis managed the Mount Crawford House tavern at the south entrance to the Notch. The inn was situated on Abel Crawford's land near today's Notchland Inn. In 1845, Davis constructed the third bridle path to the summit of Mount Washington. It was never a popular route to the mountain, and for years, in fact, it went more or less unused. It was reopened as a footpath in 1910 and now runs 14.4 miles from the south part of the Notch to a point a half-mile below Washington's summit. Davis Brook runs off the slopes of Mount Bemis, a little bit north of the Notchland Inn. Mount Davis is a 3,840-foot peak in the Montalban Ridge south of Mount Washington. Its open summit is reached via a spur trail off the Davis Path, 8.5 miles from its start off Route 302.

DISMAL POOL

Truly one of the Crawford Notch region's least known and least visited spots, this sizable pool along the upper reaches of the Saco River is less than a half-mile from the Gateway, and is usually spied only by observant motorists peering off and down to the west as they descend into the Notch from Crawford's.

Hitchcock's second volume of his massive *Geology of New Hampshire,* published in 1877, indicates the pool may have been formed by rocks and boulders blasted off Mount Willard during construction of the railroad through the Notch just a few years earlier. Up until the mid 1990s, Dismal Pool was rarely frequented

Fishermen cast their lines into seldom visited Dismal Pool at the base of Mount Willard.

(PHOTO BY AUTHOR)

as no trails to its secluded rocky shoreline existed. Its dark, dank waters (hence its name), nestled as they are in a narrow gorge at the eastern base of Mount Willard, are now more easily reached as an unmarked, unsigned trail has been brushed out from the upper parking lot nearly opposite Flume Cascade.

DRY RIVER

Also known as the Mount Washington River, the Dry River flows into the Saco River near the southern entrance of Crawford Notch State Park following a steep eight-mile journey from its source in remote Oakes Gulf, a rugged glacial cirque just to the south of Mount Washington's summit cone. The Dry River valley, much of which lies in the federally designated Presidential-Dry River Wilderness, is deep and narrow, and the upper reaches near the headwall of Oakes Gulf are spectacularly beautiful, though seldom visited by humans.

Given the nature of the river valley and its notoriety for flash flooding during times of rapid runoff, it's ironic (and perhaps intentional) that the name Dry River has been given to this scenic mountain waterway. Twice in 1971, and once in 1929, explorers of this area perished in drowning accidents. One of the 1971 victims, 16-year-old Betsey Roberts of Newton, Mass., was attempting a crossing of the rain-swollen river when she was swept 200 yards downstream in the torrent. Backpackers headed into this valley via the Dry River Trail off Route 302 should be aware of the volatility of the river and plan accordingly.

ELEPHANT HEAD

A rocky bluff forming the east side of the Gateway to the Notch, it bears an amazing resemblance to an elephant, at least when seen as one approaches the Notch from the north (or Crawford's). The top of the Elephant Head is accessed by a short, but wet spur trail off the Webster-Jackson Trail.

The bare, rocky crown of this conspicuous ledge offers superb views of the upper part of the Notch, nearby Saco Lake, and the broad, flat Crawford House site just to the north. Rock climbers are also found frequently scaling their way to the top of the Elephant Head from its base along Route 302.

The Elephant Head profile high above Route 302 near the Gateway of the Notch has long been greeting travelers to the region.

(PHOTO BY AUTHOR)

ETHAN POND:

This five-acre mountain tarn at the western base of rugged Mount Willey is named for its discoverer, legendary innkeeper, explorer, guide, woodsman, hunter, and fisherman, Ethan Allen Crawford, the famous early 19th century "Giant of the Hills." Also sometimes referred to as Willey Pond, this backcountry pond was first discovered by Crawford in 1829 and he regularly guided guests of his to its shores for a full day of trout fishing. The Appalachian Trail, which runs from Maine to Georgia, passes close by the pond. Overnight campers frequent the pond in summer and fall, taking advantage of the three-sided log lean-to and several tent platforms established off its eastern shoreline.

FIELD, MOUNT:

The highest of the peaks in the Willey Range, this 4,326-foot mountain honors Englishman Darby Field, who in 1642 became the first white man to climb to the summit of nearby 6,288-foot Mount Washington. Originally this mountain was known as Mt. Lincoln, in honor of President Abraham Lincoln. But to avoid confusion with the peak of the same name along the Franconia Range west of Crawford Notch, state geologist Charles H. Hitchcock took it upon himself to bestow a new name on the mountain.

The first trail to Mount Field's summit was cut in 1909 by a Mr. and Mrs. J.A. Cruickshank. The path was a continuation of the older Mount Avalon Trail, which ran two miles from Crawford's to the summit of Avalon. The Cruickshank's trail, known simply as the Mount Field Trail, continued southwest from Avalon to the summit of Mount Field. From there it also continued south along the ridge to neighboring Mount Willey, with this section serving as a precursor for today's Willey Range Trail.

FLUME CASCADE

The uppermost of the two waterfalls seen from Route 302 less than a half-mile below the Gateway, Flume Cascade got its name "from the singular trench through which the stream flows" as it passes under the Notch highway, wrote Moses Sweetser more than a century ago.

The cascade, or at least that portion which is seen just approaching the highway, is nothing too spectacular, unless there's been heavy rain. A more significant cascade is found a few hundred feet upstream of the roadside flume. This can be reached by a short scramble over ledges along the right shoreline of the stream, which tumbles steeply off the wooded slopes of Mount Jackson.

FRANKENSTEIN CLIFFS, Frankenstein Trestle:

The popular monster of the same name, a creation of writer Mary Shelley, is not the inspiration for the cliffs or railroad trestle which visitors see when approaching the Crawford Notch area from the south. Rather, both are named for German-born artist Godfrey Nicholas Frankenstein (1820-1873), who during the 19th century frequently visited the White Mountains, and the Crawford Notch region in particular. His interest in landscape painting was spurred, in part, by a visit to the area in 1847. Two of Frankenstein's illustrations, including one of the Crawford Notch region, appeared in William Oakes' 1848 book, *Scenery of the White Mountains.* Dr. Samuel Bemis, the Boston dentist and builder of the present-day Notchland Inn, bestowed the name of the artist on the cliffs which rise sharply out of the Saco River valley near the south entrance to the state park. Frankenstein was a frequent guest at Dr. Bemis' Crawford Notch home and a painting of Dr. Bemis, done by Frankenstein, still hangs on a wall in the Notchland Inn.

GIBBS BROOK, Gibbs Falls:

The lovely mountain stream which tumbles down the western slopes of Mount Pierce (Mount Clinton), and alongside the historic Crawford Path, is named for Col. Joseph Gibbs, early manager of the Crawford House and the Notch House. Gibbs took over management of the two Crawford Notch area hostels after Thomas Crawford was forced to relinquish both properties, due to financial hardships, in 1852. According to Frederick W. Kilbourne in his 1916 book, *Chronicles of the White Mountains*, the second Crawford House (built in 1859) was, at least for a time, known as "the Gibbs House." Gibbs, from nearby Littleton, was also the onetime proprietor of the Profile House in Franconia Notch and was known in the industry as one of the "best hotel men in New England," according to James Jackson, author of the three-volume *History of Littleton, New Hampshire*, published in 1905. Gibbs, who for years suffered from the effects of consumption, died in 1864.

HART'S LOCATION, Hart Ledge:

The town in which much of the Crawford Notch region lies, Hart's Location, is named for Colonel John Hart, who hailed from the Portsmouth area. Revolutionary War era New Hampshire Gov. John Wentworth granted the land to Hart as an apparent reward for his service in the French and Indian Wars. According to the book *New Hampshire Town Names* by Elmer Munson Hunt, the land was re-granted in 1772 to Thomas Chadbourne, also of Portsmouth. The first permanent settler in the town was young Abel Crawford, who relocated to the area from present day Bretton Woods in 1792. He is buried here near the grounds of his former mountain hostel, the Mount Crawford House, in the southern part of the Notch.

While the remote mountain hamlet is noted primarily for its scenic beauty and rugged, wild terrain, Hart's Location has for decades also been linked to the national political scene. Beginning in 1948 and continuing through the mid-1960s, the handful of year-round residents in town were always the first to cast their ballots in the first-in-the-nation New Hampshire Presidential Primary, and then also during the general election in November. Apparently weary of the national attention gained by the voting, townspeople opted to end the tradition is the late 1960s, relinquishing the honors instead to residents of tiny Dixville Notch in the northern part of the state. But in 1996, the people of Hart's Location did a turnabout and once again cast their ballots at the stroke of midnight on both election days, thus thrusting the town back into the national spotlight. Just for the record, 31 citizens cast ballots in the November general election. In the Presidential election, they gave Republican candidate Bob Dole a narrow one-vote (13-12) victory over incumbent Bill Clinton.

Hart Ledge (2,040 feet) is a prominent cliff overlooking the Saco River in Bartlett and is the southernmost peak of Bemis Ridge.

HITCHCOCK FLUME:

This narrow rock canyon on the eastern face of Mount Willard is named for its discoverer, 19th century geologist and inveterate White Mountain explorer Prof. Charles H. Hitchcock, who first found it in 1875. Moses Sweetser, author of one of the earliest White Mountain guidebooks, described the Hitchcock Flume as "a narrow canyon between high perpendicular and parallel walls of rock, its bed having a rapid slope, and being so damp as to be unsafe to venture through." Oddly, Hitchcock Flume disappeared from local maps sometime after the turn of the century, and it was "rediscovered" in the mid-1940s by Henry E. Childs, a teacher, naturalist, and longtime Appalachian Mountain Club member who recalled his search for the flume in an 1945 article, "Mount Willard Ramblings," that appeared in AMC's *Appalachia* journal (Dec. 1945).

JACKSON, MOUNT:

Although this 4,052-foot peak is considered a member peak of the Presidential Range, one would be wrong to surmise that it is named for our nation's seventh president, Andrew Jackson. Instead, former state geologist Charles Thomas Jackson, who was appointed to the post in 1838, is honored with a peak in his name. It was during an 1848 expedition on nearby Mount Clinton (or Pierce) that the mountain received its name. Moses Sweetser and other historians credit botanist William Oakes with choosing the name for the peak. Jackson, a Bostonian, supervised the first geological survey of New Hampshire in 1839-1941. Prior to coming to New Hampshire, he completed similar surveys in Maine and Rhode Island. He was also among the members of the 1840 party that accompanied Abel Crawford–then 74 years old–on the first horseback ascent of Mount Washington via the newly improved Crawford Path.

KEDRON BROOK, Kedron Flume

Situated on the southeast slope of Mount Willey, Kedron Brook flows east and joins the Saco River about a half-mile south of the Willey House site in the heart of the Notch. Besides featuring several pretty cascades, Kedron Brook passes through an interesting flume about one mile above the floor of the Notch. The flume is reached by taking the Kedron Brook Trail from the Willey House area or from a point on the Ethan Pond Trail, 1.3 miles from its start off Route 302. According to Robert and Mary Julyan, authors of *Place Names of the White Mountains*, the name of the stream and flume comes from the Bible, which references a stream of the same name "rising on the east side of Jerusalem," capital city of Israel.

NANCY BROOK, Nancy Pond, Mount Nancy, Nancy Cascades:

The tragic 1778 death of Nancy Barton–the housemaid from Jefferson who perished in the cold and snow of Crawford Notch while pursuing her husband-to-be–is memorialized in these four natural features in the southern reaches of Crawford Notch. Barton was attempting to catch up to her fiancee, who had fled with her life's savings, when she was overcome by exhaustion, plus the bitter cold of a Crawford Notch early winter storm.

The brook by which her frozen body was discovered (and which now bears her name) lies in the southern part of the Crawford Notch area, and flows eastward out of Nancy Pond, a four-acre mountain tarn at the southern base of Mount Nancy's (3,906-foot) wooded summit cone. Nancy Brook joins the Saco River a short distance south of the Notchland Inn.

The Nancy Cascades are a series of fine waterfalls which tumble some 400 feet down a steep series of ledges along the Nancy Pond Trail, 2.4 miles from Route 302.

PIERCE, MOUNT (also known as Mount Clinton):

For many years this 4,310-foot peak in the southern Presidential Range was known only as Mount Clinton, in honor of former New York City mayor and New York governor DeWitt Clinton (1769-1828). By an act of the New Hampshire legislature on April 22, 1913, however, the mountain was officially renamed Mount Pierce, to honor the only Granite State native ever elected president of the United States, Franklin Pierce (1804-1869). Although it's been more than 80 years since the renaming of the mountain, confusion still reigns over the proper name to use. For some 60 years after the name change, the Appalachian Mountain Club refused to use the peak's new name on its popular hiking maps of the region. It wasn't until the mid-1970s that AMC finally broke tradition and began listing both names on its maps. Other mapmakers, though, have been divided on the issue, and frequently list one, but not both of the names.

RIPLEY FALLS:

As is the case with many White Mountain landmarks, there is some confusion over who first discovered this lovely 100-foot high waterfall along Avalanche Brook. According to Moses Sweetser, the falls were first discovered by Abel Crawford "while out on snow-shoes, hunting sable." Thomas Starr King, in his well read book, *The White Hills*, credits Henry Wheeler Ripley of North Conway and a Mr. Porter of New York for discovering the falls after "an old fisherman had reported at the Crawford House that he had once seen a wonderful cascade on a stream that pours down" Mount Willey.

In any event, the falls were initially christened with names by Ripley and Porter (during their 1858 visit). They called the main waterfall the Sylvan-Glade Cataract, and another smaller series of falls on a side stream above, the Sparkling Cascade. Rev. Thomas Starr King, an acquaintance of Ripley, chose to rechristen the main waterfall in Ripley's name. The name Sparkling Cascade, meanwhile, has all but disappeared from use, and access to these upper cascades is restricted solely to trampers willing to bushwhack along upper sections of Avalanche Brook

ROSEBROOK RANGE, Mount Rosebrook:

Capt. Eleazar Rosebrook, father-in-law of Abel Crawford and proprietor of what was probably the first overnight hostel for travelers passing through the White Mountains, is the inspiration for the name of this ridge of mountains which runs northwest from the peaks of the Willey Range. Capt. Rosebrook, a Revolutionary War veteran, moved to the area around present-day Fabyan's in 1792 after buying out the holdings of Abel Crawford. As travel and business picked up in the Crawford's-Fabyan region following the establishment of a turnpike through Crawford Notch, Rosebrook built in 1803 a two-story house on a large mound commonly known as the "Giant's Grave." It was here that Rosebrook entertained guests quite prosperously until his death from cancer in 1817.

Mount Rosebrook, a 3,007-foot peak at the north end of the range, was once the site of a state-run forest fire lookout tower. The tower was constructed by the Bretton Woods Company in the aftermath of the disastrous Zealand Valley forest fire of 1903. Today, the mountain is the home of Bretton Woods Ski Area.

SACO LAKE, Saco River:

The name of the lake at the top of the Notch and the river which flows through the Notch on its way east to the Atlantic Ocean is derived from the Abenaki language. Saco meant "flowing out" or "outlet" in the Native American tongue, and the original Indians living along the river inhabited the area where the river flows into the ocean off the southern Maine coast.

SILVER CASCADE:

The lower of the two waterfalls on the east side of Route 302 just below the Gateway to the Notch, this sparkling mountain cascade falls one mile down Mount Webster's steep north slopes. William Oakes, in his 1848 book, *Scenery of the White Mountains,* referred to the main waterfall as the "Second Flume," as opposed to the Flume Cascade, which is viewed from the highway a quarter-mile north. Appalachian Mountain Club historian Allen Burt, writing in the June 1918 edition of *Appalachia,* said the original Silver Cascade was situated on Mount Willey, on the opposite side of the Notch, but was apparently diminished by the famous 1826 Willey Slide. At some point in the mid-1800s, the name was allowed to live on in the renaming of this spectacular waterfall, which is so impressive during the annual spring runoff, or following a period of heavy mountain rains.

Conversely, Frederick W. Kilbourne in his classic history tome, *Chronicles of the White Mountains,* credits Rev. Timothy Dwight, president of Yale University, with naming this waterfall during an autumn visit to the Notch in 1803.

TOM, MOUNT:

This 4,047-foot summit at the north end of the Willey Range is named for Thomas Jefferson Crawford, a member of the pioneering Crawford family which first settled in the Notch region two centuries ago. The son of Abel Crawford and brother of Ethan Allen Crawford, Tom Crawford operated several of the family's early mountain inns situated just above the Gateway of the Notch, and was responsible for at the least the partial construction of the first Crawford House. State geologist Charles Hitchcock bestowed the name of this legendary Crawford family member on the wooded mountain that rises just to the west of the Gateway area.

Although hikers tramping to the mountain's summit wouldn't know it today, a significant stand of virgin timber on Mount Tom's east-facing slopes was destroyed by the disastrous Hurricane of 1938. More recently, in the late 1960s and early 1970s, the mountain was under consideration as the site for a new downhill ski area planned by the last owners of the Crawford House, Littleton businessmen George McAvoy and Ambassador Robert Hill.

WEBSTER, MOUNT, Webster Cliffs:

New Hampshire born orator, lawyer and statesman Daniel Webster (1782-1852) was the inspiration for the naming of this 3,910-foot mountain which forms the eastern wall of Crawford Notch. The two-time U.S. Secretary of State was an occasional visitor to the White Mountains and the Crawford Notch-Mount Washington area in particular. In detailing a visit Webster and Ethan Allen Crawford made to the top of Mount Washington on a cold and even snowy June day in 1831, Crawford quoted Webster as saying, "Mt. Washington, I have come a long distance, and have toiled hard to arrive at your summit, and now you give me a cold reception. I am extremely sorry that I shall not have time enough to view this grand prospect which lies before me, and nothing prevents but the uncomfortable atmosphere in which you reside."

Mount Webster is considered the southernmost peak in the Presidential Range, and its slide-scarred west-facing slopes have long caught the eyes of tourists passing through the Notch. The ridgetop cliffs, which are traversed by the Appalachian Trail, provide perhaps the most unique perspective of any mountain in the immediate area.

Up until Webster's name was given to the mountaintop—reputedly by Crawford House guest Sidney Willard, a professor—the mountain was known to visitors simply as Notch Mountain.

WILLARD, MOUNT:

The Crawford Notch region's most visited mountain summit is named for either Joseph Willard, Sam Willard, or Jonathan Willard—depending upon whose historical account one wishes to believe. The 2,804-foot peak, with its breathtaking view down to the floor of the Notch, was once known as Mount Tom; a name given it by Prof. Tuckerman following an 1844 visit to its summit. He named the peak for local innkeeper Thomas Crawford, who constructed the first carriage road to the mountain's summit in 1846.

It is unclear who changed the name to Mount Willard, and who is the inspiration for the name. Sweetser wrote that some old accounts reveal it was named for Harvard University professor Sidney Willard, while a more accepted account says Joseph Willard of Boston, an admirer of the mountain's summit view, inspired the name change by Tom Crawford himself, who had accompanied Willard on a hike to the summit.

Other highly suspicious accounts claim the mountain may have been named for a reclusive North Country hunter from Lancaster, Jonathan Willard, for whom several natural landmarks in the northern White Mountains are named. His connection to the Crawford Notch area is dubious at best since all indications are he spent the majority of his time in the region living in solitude in the dense forest at the foot of the Kilkenny mountain range east of Lancaster.

WILLEY, MOUNT, Willey Pond, Willey Brook, Willey Range:

The Crawford Notch region's second most famous family—that of settler Sam Willey—live in infamy through the various local landmarks that today bear their name. The tragic death of the Willey clan during an August 26, 1826 rainstorm is perhaps the region's most oft told tale. The Willeys lived in a small cabin at the floor of the Notch, and following a day of torrential rains, were killed while attempting to flee a massive landslide which came rumbling down the mountain that now bears their name.

Mount Willey is the 4,302-foot peak that serves as the western wall to Crawford Notch. It was first climbed in 1845 by Prof. Edward Tuckerman. The name Willey Pond has been bestowed on the man-made pond along the Saco River directly across from the Willey House site; it is also an alternate name for Ethan Pond on the west side of Mount Willey. Willey Brook tumbles down off the Willey Range mountains north of Mount Willey in the ravine separating that mountain from neighboring Mount Field.

SIXTEEN

Bibliography and Historical Sources

Many sources were used in preparing this overview of the Crawford Notch area. While the following list is far from complete, those interested in delving more deeply into the lore of Crawford Notch and the entire White Mountain region will find much of interest in the works mentioned below.

GEOLOGY and NATURAL HISTORY

Audubon Society of New Hampshire. A Brief Guide to the Natural History of the White Mountains. *Concord, NH: 1967 (out of print).*

Beecher, Ned. Outdoor Explorations in Mt. Washington Valley. *Conway, NH: Tin Mountain Conservation Center, 1989.*

Billings, Marland P. et. al. Geology of the Mt. Washington Quadrangle. *Reprint. Concord, NH: New Hampshire Department of Resources and Economic Development, 1979*

Bliss, L.C., Alpine Zone of the Presidential Range. *1963.*

Henderson, Donald M. et al. Geology of the Crawford Notch Quadrangle. *Concord, NH: New Hampshire Department of Resources and Economic Development, 1977.*

Raymo, Chet and Maureen E. Written in Stone: A Geological History of the Northeastern United States. *Old Saybrook, CT: The Globe Pequot Press, 1989.*

Reifsnyder, William E. High Huts of the White Mountains. *2nd edition, Boston: Appalachian Mountain Club, 1993.*

PLANTS

Harris, Stuart K., Langerheim, Jean, and Steele, Frederic. AMC Field Guide to Mountain Flowers of New England. *2nd edition. Boston: Appalachian Mountain Club, 1977.*

Marchand, Peter J. North Woods: An Inside Look at the Nature of Forests in the Northeast. *Boston: Appalachian Mountain Club, 1987.*

Steele, Frederic L. At Timberline: A Nature Guide to the Mountains of the Northeast. *Boston: Appalachian Mountain Club, 1982.*

Slack, Nancy D. and Bell, Allison W. Field Guide to the New England Alpine Summits. *Boston: Appalachian Mountain Club, 1995.*

WILDLIFE

Delovey, Alan. A Birder's Guide to New Hampshire. *Colorado Springs, CO: American Birding Association, 1996.*

Foss, Carol R. ed. Atlas of Breeding Birds in New Hampshire. *Concord, NH: New Hampshire Audubon Society, 1994.*

White Mountain National Forest. Checklist for Birds. *Laconia. NH.*

HIKING/CLIMBING

Bolnick, Bruce and Doreen. Waterfalls of the White Mountains. *Woodstock, VT: Backcountry Publications, 1990.*

Buschbaum, Robert N. Nature Hikes in the White Mountains. *Boston: Appalachian Mountain Club, 1995.*

Daniell , Eugene S. III, ed. AMC White Mountain Guide. *25th edition. Boston: Appalachian Mountain Club, 1992.*

Doan, Daniel. Fifty Hikes in the White Mountains. *4th edition. Woodstock, VT: Backcountry Publications, 1990.*

Doan, Daniel. Fifty More Hikes in New Hampshire. *3rd edition. Woodstock, VT: Backcountry Publications, 1991.*

Emblidge, David, ed. The Appalachian Trail Reader. *London, Oxford University Press, 1996.*

Luxenberg, Larry. Walking the Appalachian Trail. *Mechanicsburg, PA: Stackpole Books, 1994.*

Schofield, Bruce. High Peaks of the Northeast. *North Amherst, MA: New England Cartographics, 1993.*

Scudder, Brent E. Scudder's White Mountain Viewing Guide. *Bellmore, NY: High Top Press, 1995.*

Smith, Steven D. Ponds and Lakes of the White Mountains. *Woodstock, VT: Backcountry Publications, 1993.*

Webster, Ed. Rock Climbs in the White Mountains of New Hampshire. *3rd Edition. Eldorado Springs, CO: Mountain Imagery, 1993.*

Wilcox, Rick. An Ice Climber's Guide to Northern New England. *2nd Edition. North Conway, NH: International Mountain Equipment, Inc., 1992.*

HISTORY/GENERAL INTEREST

Belcher, C. Francis. Logging Railroads of the White Mountains. *Boston: Appalachian Mountain Club, 1980.*

Burt, F. Allen. The Story of Mt. Washington. *Hanover, NH: Dartmouth Publications, 1960 (out of print).*

Carroll, Aileen. Bartlett, New Hampshire...in the valley of the Saco. *West Kennebunk, ME: Phoenix Publishing, 1990.*

Casanave, Suki. Natural Wonders of New Hampshire. *Castine, ME: Country Roads Press, 1994.*

Downs, Virginia. Life by the tracks. *Canaan, NH: Phoenix Publishing, 1983.*

Hancock, Frances Ann Johnson. Crawford Notch in the White Mountains. *Littleton, NH: Courier Printing Company. Circa 1965.*

Julyan, Robert and Mary. The Place Names of the White Mountains. *Revised edition. Hanover, NH: University Press of New England, 1993.*

Johnson, Ron, ed. Maine Central Railroad Mountain Division. *Portland, Maine: 470 Railroad Club, 1986.*

McAvoy, George. And Then There Was One: A History of the Hotels of the Summit and the West Side of Mt. Washington. *Littleton, NH: The Crawford Press, 1988.*

Morse, Stearns, ed. Lucy Crawford's History of the White Mountains. *Boston: Appalachian Mountain Club, 1978.*

Mudge, John T.B. The White Mountains: Names, Places and Legends. *Etna, NH: The Durand Press, 1992.*

New Hampshire Historical Society, The Grand Resort Hotels and Tourism in the White Mountains. *Concord, NH: 1995.*

Ramsey, Floyd W. Shrouded Memories: True Stories from the White Mountains of New Hampshire. *Littleton, NH: 1994.*

Robertson, Edwin B. and English, Benjamin W. Jr. A Century of Railroading in Crawford Notch. *1996 edition. Westbrook, ME: Robertson Books, 1996.*

Robertson, Edwin. B. Building the Railroad Through Crawford Notch. *Westbrook, ME: Robertson Books, 1996.*

Rowan, Peter and June Hammond, ed. Mountain Summers. *Randolph, NH: Gulfside Press, 1995.*

Stier, Maggie and McAdow, Ron. Into the Mountains. *Boston: Appalachian Mountain Club, 1995.*

Waterman, Laura and Guy. Forest and Crag: A History of Hiking, Trailblazing and Adventure in the Northeast Mountains. *Boston: Appalachian Mountain Club, 1989.*

CLASSICS and/or OUT OF PRINT

Drake, Samuel A. The Heart of the White Mountains. *New York: Harper and Brothers, 1882.*

Eastman, Samuel .C. The White Mountain Guidebook. *7th edition. Boston, Lee and Shepard, 1867.*

Hunt, Elmer Munson. New Hampshire Town Names. *Peterborough, NH: 1970.*

Jackson, James R. History of Littleton, New Hampshire. *Littleton, NH: 1905*

Keyes, George L. Keyes' Handbook of Northern Pleasure Travel. *Boston: 1873.*

Kilbourne, Frederick W. Chronicles of the White Mountains. *Boston. Houghton Mifflin Company, 1916.*

King, Thomas Starr. The White Hills, Their Legends, Landscape and Poetry. *Boston: Crosby and Ainsworth, 1859.*

Oakes, William, Scenery of the White Mountains. *Boston: 1848.*

Somer, Rev. A.N., History of Lancaster. *Concord, NH: 1899.*

Spaulding, James H., Historical Relics of the White Mountains. *Boston: 1855.*

Sweetser, Moses F., The White Mountains: A Handbook for Travelers, *4th edition. Boston, James R. Osgood, 1881. 14th edition. Boston: Houghton, Mifflin and Company, 1896.*

Sweetser, Moses F. A Guide to the White Mountains. *Boston: Houghton Mifflin Company, 1918.*

Sweetser, Moses. F. Chisholm's White Mountain Guide. *1902 edition. Portland, ME: Chisholm Brothers.*

Ward, Julius H. The White Mountains: A Guide to Their Interpretation. *New York: D. Appleton and Co., 1890.*

Willey, Benjamin. Incidents in White Mountain History. *Boston: 1856.*

About the Authors

MIKE DICKERMAN is an award winning writer and photographer for *The Courier* newspaper of Littleton, N.H. His popular hiking column, "The beaten path," earned him 1995 Sports Columnist of the Year honors by the New Hampshire Press Association. A collection of his hiking stories, *Along the Beaten Path*, was published in 1994 and is in its third printing. A second collection of his columns is due to be published in the fall of 1997. He and his wife, Jeanne, reside in Littleton.

STEVE SMITH has been hiking and exploring the White Mountains of New Hampshire for nearly two decades. He has written numerous pieces on hiking and area history for several publications, including AMC's *Appalachia Journal*. He is also the author of *Ponds and Lakes of the White Mountains: From Wayside to Wilderness*, published in 1993 by Backcountry Publications of Woodstock, Vt. Smith lives in Lincoln, N.H.

JOHN DICKERMAN is manager of Crawford Notch State Park, where he has worked each summer since 1983. His hiking days in the White Mountains go back 20 years or more. Like his coauthors, he's also a former Mount Washington Hotel employee. Dickerman, his wife, Jane, and their two children, Garth and Thea, live in Bethlehem, N.H.